Planet Earth

1 0 0 0 F A C T S

John Farndon

Consultant Peter Riley

Miles Kelly
PUBLISHING

Planet
Earth

1 0 0 0   F A C T S

This material was first published as hardback in 2002 by Bardfield Press
Bardfield Press is an imprint of Miles Kelly Publishing Ltd
Bardfield Centre, Great Bardfield, Essex, CM7 4SL

This edition published in 2007 by Miles Kelly Publishing Ltd

2 4 6 8 10 9 7 5 3 1

Editorial Director: Belinda Gallagher
Art Director: Jo Brewer
Assistant Editor: Lucy Dowling
Design: WhiteLight
Picture Researcher: Liberty Newton
Production Manager: Elizabeth Brunwin
Reprographics: Anthony Cambray, Liberty Newton

British Library Cataloguing-in-Publication Data
A catalogue record for this book is available from the British Library

ISBN 978-1-84236-936-4

Printed in China

www.mileskelly.net
info@mileskelly.net

Contents

PLANET EARTH

VOLCANOES AND EARTHQUAKES

Contents

SHAPING THE LAND

WEATHER AND CLIMATE

CONTINENTS

OCEANS

Formation of the Earth

- **The Earth formed** 4.57 billion years ago out of debris left over from the explosion of a giant star.

- **The Earth began to form** as star debris spun round the newly formed Sun and clumped into rocks called planetesimals.

- **Planetesimals** were pulled together by their own gravity to form planets such as Earth and Mars.

- **At first** the Earth was a seething mass of molten rock.

- **After 50 million years** a giant rock cannoned into the newborn Earth. The impact melted the rock into a hot splash, which cooled to become our Moon.

- **The shock of the impact** that formed the Moon made iron and nickel collapse towards the Earth's centre. They formed a core so dense that its atoms fuse in nuclear reactions that have kept the inside of the Earth hot ever since.

- **The molten rock** formed a thick mantle about 3000 km thick around the metal core. The core's heat keeps the mantle warm and churning, like boiling porridge.

- **After about 100 million years** the surface of the mantle cooled and hardened to form a thin crust.

- **Steam and gases** billowing from volcanoes formed the Earth's first, poisonous atmosphere.

- **After 200 million years** the steam had condensed to water. It fell in huge rain showers to form the oceans.

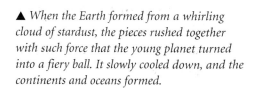

▲ *When the Earth formed from a whirling cloud of stardust, the pieces rushed together with such force that the young planet turned into a fiery ball. It slowly cooled down, and the continents and oceans formed.*

9

The Ages of the Earth

- **The Earth formed 4570 million years ago** (**mya**) but the first animals with shells and bones appeared less than 600 mya. It is mainly with the help of their fossils that geologists have learned about the Earth's history since then. We know very little about the 4000 million years before, known as Precambrian Time.

- **Just as days are divided** into hours and minutes, so geologists divide the Earth's history into time periods. The longest are eons, thousands of millions of years long. The shortest are chrons, a few thousand years long. In between come eras, periods, epochs and ages.

- **The years since Precambrian Time** are split into three eras: Palaeozoic, Mesozoic and Cenozoic.

- **Different plants and animals** lived at different times, so geologists can tell from the fossils in rocks how long ago the rocks formed. Using fossils, they have divided the Earth's history since Precambrian Time into 11 periods.

2 mya

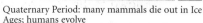

Quaternary Period: many mammals die out in Ice Ages; humans evolve

65 mya

Tertiary Period: first large mammals; birds flourish; widespread grasslands

144 mya

Cretaceous Period: first flowering plants; the dinosaurs die out

213 mya

Jurassic Period: dinosaurs widespread; Archaeopteryx, earliest known bird

248 mya

Triassic Period: first mammals; seed-bearing plants spread; Europe is in the tropics

286 mya

Permian Period: conifers replace ferns as big trees; deserts are widespread

- **Layers of rock** form on top of each other, so the oldest rocks are usually at the bottom and the youngest at the top, unless they have been disturbed. The order of layers from top to bottom is known as the geological column.

- **By looking for certain fossils** geologists can tell if one layer of rock is older than another.

- **Fossils can only show** if a rock is older or younger than another; they cannot give a date in years. Also, many rocks such as igneous rocks contain no fossils. To give an absolute date, geologists may use radiocarbon dating.

- **Radiocarbon dating** allows the oldest rocks on Earth to be dated. After certain substances, such as uranium and rubidium, form in rocks, their atoms slowly break down into different atoms. As atoms break down they send out rays, or radioactivity. By assessing how many atoms in a rock have changed, geologists work out the rock's age.

- **Breaks in the sequence** of the geological column are called unconformities.

360 mya

Carboniferous Period: vast warm swamps of fern forests which form coal; first reptiles

408 mya

Devonian Period: first insects and amphibians; ferns and mosses as big as trees

438 mya

Silurian Period: first land plants; fish with jaws and freshwater fish

505 mya

Ordovician Period: early fish-like vertebrates appear; the Sahara is glaciated

590 mya

Cambrian Period: no life on land, but shellfish flourish in the oceans

Precambrian Time: the first life forms (bacteria) appear, and give the air oxygen

11

Shape of the Earth

- **The study of the shape of the Earth** is called geodesy. In the past, geodesy depended on ground-based surveys. Today, satellites play a major role.

- **The Earth is not a perfect sphere.** It is a unique shape called a geoid, which means 'Earth shaped'.

- **The Earth spins** faster at the Equator than at the Poles, because the Equator is farther from the Earth's spinning axis.

- **The extra speed** of the Earth at the Equator flings it out in a bulge, while it is flattened at the Poles.

▲ *The ancient Greeks realized that the Earth is a globe. Satellite measurements show that it is not quite perfectly round.*

- **Equatorial bulge** was predicted in 1687 by Isaac Newton.

  The equatorial bulge was confirmed 70 years after Newton – by French surveys in Peru by Charles de La Condamine, and in Lapland by Pierre de Maupertuis.

- **The Earth's diameter** at the Equator is 12,758 km. This is larger, by 43 km, than the vertical diameter from North Pole to South Pole.

- **The official measurement** of the Earth's radius at the Equator is 6,376,136 m plus or minus 1 m.

- **The Lageos** (Laser Geodynamic) satellite launched in 1976 has measured gravitational differences with extreme precision. It has revealed bumps up to 100 m high, notably just south of India.

- **The Seasat** satellite confirmed the ocean surfaces are geoid. It took millions of measurements of the height of the ocean surface, accurate to within a few centimetres.

Axis

North pole

South pole

▶ *The Earth rotates around its axis, the imaginary line running through the centre of the planet from pole to pole at an angle of 23.5°.*

13

The Earth's chemistry

- **The bulk of the Earth** is made from iron, oxygen, magnesium and silicon.

- **More than 80 chemical elements** occur naturally in the Earth and its atmosphere.

- **The crust** is made mostly from oxygen and silicon, with aluminium, iron, calcium, magnesium, sodium, potassium, titanium and traces of 64 other elements.

- **The upper mantle** is made up of iron and magnesium silicates; the lower is silicon and magnesium sulphides and oxides.

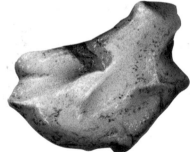

- **The core** is mostly iron, with a little nickel and traces of sulphur, carbon, oxygen and potassium.

- **Evidence for the Earth's chemistry** comes from analysing densities with the help of earthquake waves, and from studying stars, meteorites and other planets.

▲ *Zircon crystals found in Australia were 4276 million years old – the oldest part of the Earth's crust ever discovered.*

- **When the Earth** was still semi-molten, dense elements such as iron sank to form the core. Lighter elements such as oxygen floated up to form the crust.

- **Some heavy elements,** such as uranium, ended up in the crust because they easily make compounds with oxygen and silicon.
- **Large blobs of elements** that combine easily with sulphur, such as zinc and lead, spread through the mantle.
- **Elements that combine with iron,** such as gold and nickel, sank to the core.

▼ *This diagram shows the percentages of the chemical elements that make up the Earth.*

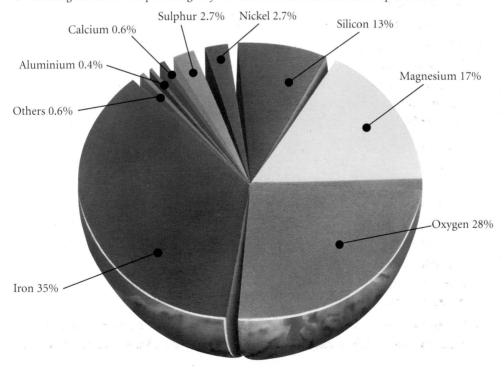

Sulphur 2.7%   Nickel 2.7%   Silicon 13%

Calcium 0.6%

Aluminium 0.4%

Magnesium 17%

Others 0.6%

Oxygen 28%

Iron 35%

Earth's interior

- **The Earth's crust** (see crust) is a thin hard outer shell of rock which is a few dozen kilometres thick. Its thickness in relation to the Earth is about the same as the skin on an apple.

- **Under the crust,** there is a deep layer of hot soft rock called the mantle (see core and mantle).

- **The crust and upper mantle** can be divided into three layers according to their rigidity: the lithosphere, the asthenosphere and the mesosphere.

- **Beneath the mantle** is a core of hot iron and nickel. The outer core is so hot – climbing from 4500°C to 6000°C – that it is always molten. The inner core is even hotter (up to 7000°C) but it stays solid because the pressure is 6000 times greater than on the surface.

- **The inner core** contains 1.7% of the Earth's mass, the outer core 30.8%; the core–mantle boundary 3%; the lower mantle 49%; the upper mantle 15%; the ocean crust 0.099% and the continental crust 0.374%.

- **Satellite measurements** are so accurate they can detect slight lumps and dents in the Earth's surface. These indicate where gravity is stronger or weaker because of differences in rock density. Variations in gravity reveal things such as mantle plumes (see hot-spot volcanoes).

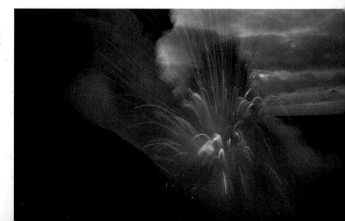

▶ *Hot material from the Earth's interior often bursts on to the surface from volcanoes.*

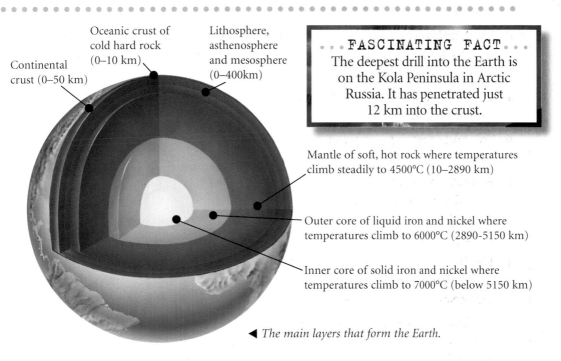

Continental crust (0–50 km)

Oceanic crust of cold hard rock (0–10 km)

Lithosphere, asthenosphere and mesosphere (0–400km)

...FASCINATING FACT...
The deepest drill into the Earth is on the Kola Peninsula in Arctic Russia. It has penetrated just 12 km into the crust.

Mantle of soft, hot rock where temperatures climb steadily to 4500°C (10–2890 km)

Outer core of liquid iron and nickel where temperatures climb to 6000°C (2890-5150 km)

Inner core of solid iron and nickel where temperatures climb to 7000°C (below 5150 km)

◀ *The main layers that form the Earth.*

- **Our knowledge of the Earth's interior** comes mainly from studying how earthquake waves move through different kinds of rock.

- **Analysis of how earthquake waves** are deflected reveals where different materials occur in the interior. S (secondary) waves pass only through the mantle. P (primary) waves pass through the core as well. P waves passing through the core are deflected, leaving a shadow zone where no waves reach the far side of the Earth.

- **The speed of earthquake waves** reveals how dense the rocky materials are. Cold, hard rock transmits waves more quickly than hot, soft rock.

17

The lithosphere

- **The lithosphere** is the upper, rigid layer of the Earth. It consists of the crust and the top of the mantle (see core and mantle). It is about 100 km thick.

- **The lithosphere** was discovered by 'seismology', which means listening to the pattern of vibrations from earthquakes.

- **Fast earthquake waves** show that the top of the mantle is as rigid as the crust, although chemically it is different.

- **Lithosphere** means 'ball of stone'.

- **The lithosphere** is broken into 20 or so slabs, called tectonic plates. The continents sit on top of these plates (see continental drift).

▲ *The hard rocky surface of the Earth is made up of the 20 or so strong rigid plates of the lithosphere.*

- **Temperatures** increase by 35°C for every 1000 m you move down through the lithosphere.

- **Below the lithosphere,** in the Earth's mantle, is the hot, soft rock of the asthenosphere (see Earth's interior).

- **The boundary between the lithosphere** and the asthenosphere occurs at the point where temperatures climb above 1300°C.

- **The lithosphere** is only a few kilometres thick under the middle of the oceans. Here, the mantle's temperature just below the surface is 1300°C.

- **The lithosphere is thickest** – 120 km or so – under the continents.

▲ *The Earth's crust is thin and rocky. All areas of wet and dry land are part of this crust, including the ocean floor.*

Crust

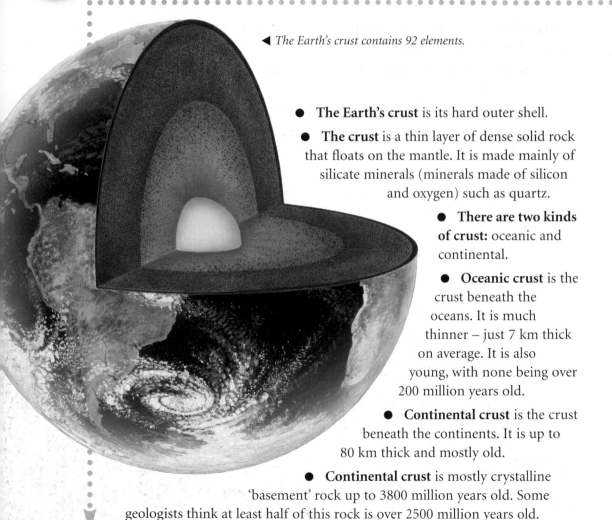

◀ *The Earth's crust contains 92 elements.*

- **The Earth's crust** is its hard outer shell.

- **The crust** is a thin layer of dense solid rock that floats on the mantle. It is made mainly of silicate minerals (minerals made of silicon and oxygen) such as quartz.

- **There are two kinds of crust:** oceanic and continental.

- **Oceanic crust** is the crust beneath the oceans. It is much thinner – just 7 km thick on average. It is also young, with none being over 200 million years old.

- **Continental crust** is the crust beneath the continents. It is up to 80 km thick and mostly old.

- **Continental crust** is mostly crystalline 'basement' rock up to 3800 million years old. Some geologists think at least half of this rock is over 2500 million years old.

- **It is estimated** that approximately one cubic kilometre of new continental crust is probably being created each year.

- **The 'basement' rock** has two main layers: an upper half of silica-rich rocks such as granite, schist and gneiss, and a lower half of volcanic rocks such as basalt which have less silica. Ocean crust is mostly basalt.

- **Continental crust** is created in the volcanic arcs above subduction zones (see converging plates). Molten rock from the subducted plate oozes to the surface over a period of a few hundred thousand years.

- **The boundary** between the crust and the mantle beneath it is called the Mohorovicic discontinuity.

▶ *The Horn of Africa and the Red Sea is one of the places where the Earth's thin oceanic crust is cracked and moving. It is gradually widening the Red Sea.*

Core and mantle

- **The mantle** makes up the bulk of the Earth's interior. It reaches from about 10–90 km to 2890 km down.

- **As you move** through the mantle temperatures climb steadily, until they reach 3000°C.

- **Mantle rock** is so warm that it churns slowly round like very, very thick treacle boiling on a stove. This movement is known as mantle convection currents.

- **Mantle rock moves** about 10,000 times more slowly than the hour hand on a kitchen clock. Cooler mantle rock takes about 200 million years to sink all the way to the core.

- **Near the surface,** mantle rock may melt into floods of magma. These may gush through the upper layers like oil that is being squeezed from a sponge.

- **The boundary** between the mantle and the core (see Earth's interior) is called the core–mantle boundary (CMB).

- **The CMB** is about 250 km thick. It is an even more dramatic change than between the ground and the air.

- **Temperatures jump by 1500°C** at the CMB.

- **The difference** in density between the core and the mantle at the CMB is twice as great as the difference between air and rock.

▶ *Every now and then, mantle rock melts into floods of magma, which collects along the edges of tectonic plates. It then rises to the surface and erupts as a volcano.*

...FASCINATING FACT...
Scientists have found 'anti-continents' on the
CMB that match with continents on the surface.

Converging plates

▲ *Volcanoes in subduction zones are usually highly explosive. This is because the magma becomes contaminated as it burns its way up through the continental crust.*

- **In many places** around the world, the tectonic plates that make up the Earth's crust, or outer layer, are slowly crunching together with enormous force.

- **The Atlantic** is getting wider, pushing the Americas further west. Yet the Earth is not getting any bigger because as the American plates crash into the Pacific plates, the thinner, denser ocean plates are driven down into the Earth's hot mantle and are destroyed.

- **The process** of driving an ocean plate down into the Earth's interior is called subduction.

...**FASCINATING FACT**...
Subduction creates a ring of volcanoes around the Pacific Ocean called the 'Ring of Fire'.

- **Subduction** creates deep ocean trenches typically 6–7 km deep at the point of collision. One of these, the Mariana Trench, could drown Mt Everest with 2 km to spare on top.

- **As an ocean plate** bends down into the Earth's mantle, it cracks. The movement of these cracks sets off earthquakes originating up to 700 km down. These earthquake zones are called Benioff–Wadati zones after Hugo Benioff, who discovered them in the 1950s.

- **As an ocean plate** slides down, it melts and makes blobs of magma. This magma floats up towards the surface, punching its way through to create a line of volcanoes along the edge of the continental plate.

- **If volcanoes in subduction zones** emerge in the sea, they form a curving line of volcanic islands called an island arc. Beyond this arc is the back-arc basin, an area of shallow sea that slowly fills up with sediments.

- **As a subducting plate sinks,** the continental plate scrapes sediments off the ocean plate and piles them in a great wedge. Between this wedge and the island arc there may be a fore-arc basin, which is a shallow sea that slowly fills with sediment.

- **Where two continental plates collide,** the plate splits into two layers: a lower layer of dense mantle rock and an upper layer of lighter crustal rock, which is too buoyant to be subducted. As the mantle rock goes down, the crustal rock peels off and crumples against the other to form fold mountains (see mountain ranges).

▼ *This is a cross-section through the top 1000 km or so of the Earth's surface. It shows a subduction zone, where an ocean plate is bent down beneath a continental plate.*

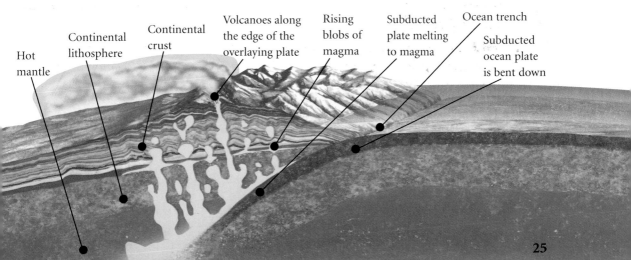

Hot mantle

Continental lithosphere

Continental crust

Volcanoes along the edge of the overlaying plate

Rising blobs of magma

Subducted plate melting to magma

Ocean trench

Subducted ocean plate is bent down

25

Diverging plates

- **Deep down on the ocean floor,** some of the tectonic plates of the Earth's crust are slowly pushing apart. New molten rock wells up from the mantle into the gap between them and freezes onto their edges. As plates are destroyed at subduction zones, so new plate spreads the ocean floor wider.

- **The spreading of the ocean floor** centres on ridges down the middle of some oceans, mid-ocean ridges. Some of these ridges link up to make the world's longest mountain range, winding over 60,000 km beneath the oceans.

- **The Mid-Atlantic Ridge** stretches through the Atlantic from North Pole to South Pole. The East Pacific Rise winds under the Pacific Ocean from Mexico to Antarctica.

- **Along the middle** of a mid-ocean ridge is a deep canyon. This is where molten rock from the mantle wells up through the sea-bed.

▼ *This is a cross-section of the top 50 km or so of the Earth's surface. It shows where the sea floor is spreading away from the mid-ocean ridge.*

Mantle

Transform fault

Central canyon

Mid-ocean ridge

Magma erupts through the gap as lava solidifies into new sea floor

Ocean plate

Ridges are lower and older away from the centre

- **Mid-ocean ridges** are broken by the curve of the Earth's surface into short stepped sections. Each section is marked off by a long sideways crack called a transform fault. As the sea floor spreads out from a ridge, the sides of the fault rub together setting off earthquakes.

- **As molten rock wells** up from a ridge and freezes, its magnetic material sets in a certain way to line up with the Earth's magnetic field. Because the field reverses every now and then, bands of material set in alternate directions. This means that scientists can see how the sea floor has spread in the past.

▲ *Unlike subduction zones, which create explosive volcanoes, diverging plates create volcanoes that ooze lava gently. For this to happen above the ocean surface is rare.*

- **Rates of sea floor spreading** vary from 1 cm to 20 cm a year. Slow-spreading ridges such as the Mid-Atlantic Ridge are much higher, with seamounts often topping the ridge. Fast-spreading ridges such as the East Pacific Rise are lower, and magma oozes from these just like surface fissure volcanoes.

- **Hot magma** bubbling up through a mid-ocean ridge emerges as hot lava. As it comes into contact with the cold seawater it freezes into blobs, pillow lava.

- **Mid-ocean ridges** may begin where a mantle plume (see hot-spot volcanoes) rises through the mantle and melts through the sea-bed.

...FASCINATING FACT...
About 10 cubic km of new crust is created
at the mid-ocean ridges every year.

Tectonic plates

- **The Earth's surface** is divided into slabs called tectonic plates. Each plate is a fragment of the Earth's rigid outer layer, or lithosphere (see the lithosphere).

- **There are 16 large plates** and several smaller ones. Plates are approximately 100 km thick but can vary in thickness from 8 km to 200 km.

- **The biggest plate** is the Pacific plate, which underlies the whole of the Pacific Ocean. The Pacific Ocean represents half of the world's ocean area.

- **Tectonic plates** are moving all the time – by about 10 cm a year. Over hundreds of millions of years they move vast distances. Some have moved halfway round the globe.

- **The continents** are embedded in the tops of the plates, so as the plates move the continents move with them.

- **The Pacific plate** is the only large plate with no part of a continent situated on it. It represents more than one-third of the Earth's surface area.

- **The movement** of tectonic plates accounts for many things, including the pattern of volcanic and earthquake activity around the world.

▲ *Beneath the Pacific Ocean lies the Pacific plate, the largest of the tectonic plates.*

- **There are three kinds** of boundary between plates: convergent, divergent and transform.

- **Tectonic plates** are probably driven by convection currents of molten rock that circulate within the Earth's mantle (see core and mantle).

- **The lithosphere** was too thin for tectonic plates until 500 million years ago.

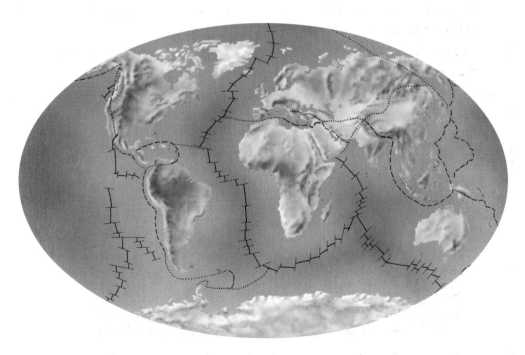

▲ *This map shows some of the jagged boundaries between plates.*

29

Faults

- **A fault** is a fracture in rock along which large blocks of rock have slipped past each other.

- **Faults usually occur** in fault zones, which are often along the boundaries between tectonic plates. Faults are typically caused by earthquakes.

- **Single earthquakes** rarely move blocks more than a few centimetres. Repeated small earthquakes can shift blocks hundreds of kilometres.

- **Compression faults** are faults caused by rocks being squeezed together, perhaps by converging plates.

- **Tension faults** are faults caused by rocks being pulled together, perhaps by diverging plates.

- **Normal, or dip-slip, faults** are tension faults where the rock fractures and slips straight down.

▲ *Unlike most faults the San Andreas Fault in California is visible on the Earth's surface.*

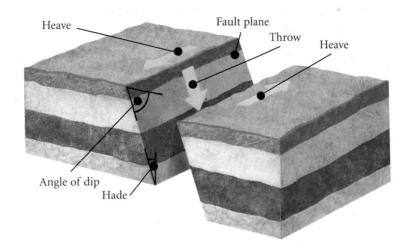

Geologists who study faults describe the movement of a fault using the terms illustrated here.

- **A wrench, or tear, fault** occurs when plates slide past each other and make blocks slip horizontally.

- **Large wrench faults,** such as the San Andreas in California, USA, are called transcurrent faults.

- **Rift valleys** are huge, trough-shaped valleys created by faulting, such as Africa's Great Rift Valley. The floor is a thrown-down block called a graben. Some geologists think they are caused by tension, others by compression.

- **Horst blocks** are blocks of rock thrown up between normal faults, often creating a high plateau.

Folds

- **Rocks usually form** in flat layers called strata. Tectonic plates can collide (see converging plates) with such force that they crumple up these strata.

- **Sometimes the folds** are just tiny wrinkles a few centimetres long. Sometimes they are gigantic, with hundreds of kilometres between crests (the highest points on a fold).

- **The shape of a fold** depends on the force that is squeezing it and on the resistance of the rock.

- **The slope of a fold** is called the dip. The direction of the dip is the direction in which it is sloping.

- **The strike of the fold** is at right angles to the dip. It is the horizontal alignment of the fold.

- **Some folds turn right over** on themselves to form upturned folds called nappes.

◀ *The Alps in Europe are fold mountains. They formed when two of the Earth's plates collided. This collision caused layers of rocks to crumple and fold.*

- **As nappes fold on top of other nappes,** the crumpled strata may pile up into mountains.

- **A downfold** is called a syncline; an upfolded arch of strata is called an anticline.

- **The axial plane** of a fold divides the fold into halves.

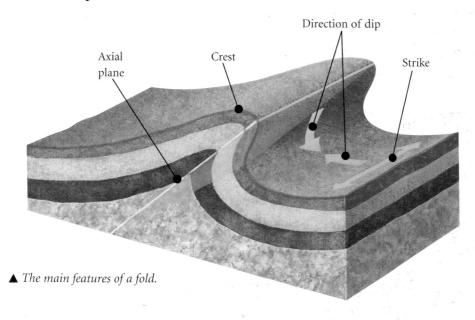

▲ *The main features of a fold.*

Direction of dip

Axial plane

Crest

Strike

...FASCINATING FACT...
Most of the world's oil comes from
reservoirs that are trapped in anticlines.

Rocks

▲ *The Kent coast near Dover is famous for its white cliffs which are made of chalk.*

● **The oldest known rocks** on Earth are 3900 million years old – they are the Acasta gneiss rocks from Canada.

● **There are three main kinds of rock:** igneous rock, sedimentary rock and metamorphic rock.

● **Igneous rocks** (igneous means 'fiery') are made when hot molten magma or lava cools and solidifies.

- **Volcanic rocks,** such as basalt, are igneous rocks that form from lava that has erupted from volcanoes.

- **Metamorphic rocks** are rocks that have changed over time, such as limestone which is made into marble because of the heat generated by magma.

- **Sedimentary rocks** are rocks that are made from the slow hardening of sediments into layers, or strata.

- **Some sedimentary rocks,** such as sandstone, are made from sand and silt. Other rocks are broken down into these materials by weathering and erosion.

- **Most sediments** form on the sea-bed. Sand is washed down onto the sea-bed by rivers.

- **Limestone and chalk** are sedimentary rocks made mainly from the remains of sea creatures.

▶ *Rocks are continually recycled. Whether they form from volcanoes or sediments, all rocks are broken down into sand by weathering and erosion. The sand is deposited on sea-beds and river-beds where it hardens to form new rock. This process is the rock cycle.*

Fossils

▼ *Scientists study fossils to learn about the Earth's history and about the animals and plants that lived millions of years ago.*

- **Fossils** are the remains of living things preserved for millions of years, usually in stone.

- **Most fossils** are the remains of living things such as bones, shells, eggs, leaves and seeds.

- **Trace fossils** are fossils of signs left behind by creatures, such as footprints and scratch marks.

- **Paleontologists** (scientists who study fossils) tell the age of a fossil from the rock layer in which it is found. Also, they measure how the rock has changed radioactively since it was formed (radiocarbon dating).

- **The oldest fossils** are called stromatolites. They are fossils of big, pizza-like colonies of microscopic bacteria over 3500 million years old.

▶ *When an animal dies, its soft parts rot away quickly. If its bones or shell are buried quickly in mud, they may turn to stone. When a shellfish such as this ancient trilobite dies and sinks to the sea-bed, its shell is buried. Over millions of years, water trickling through the mud may dissolve the shell, but minerals in the water fill its place to make a perfect cast.*

- **The biggest fossils** are conyphytons, 2000-million-year-old stromatolites over 100 m high.

- **Not all fossils** are stone. Mammoths have been preserved by being frozen in the permafrost (see cold landscapes) of Siberia.

- **Insects** have been preserved in amber, the solidified sap of ancient trees.

- **Certain widespread, short-lived fossils** are very useful for dating rock layers. These are known as index fossils.

- **Index fossils** include ancient shellfish such as trilobites, graptolites, crinoids, belemnites, ammonites and brachiopods.

1. A trilobite dies on the ocean floor long ago.

2. The trilobite's soft parts eventually rot away.

3. The shell is slowly buried by mud.

4. Mineral-rich waters dissolve the shell.

5. New minerals fill the mould to form a fossil.

37

Minerals

- **Minerals** are the natural chemicals from which rocks are made.

- **All but a few minerals** are crystals.

- **Some rocks are made** from crystals of just one mineral; many are made from half a dozen or more minerals.

- **Most minerals** are combinations of two or more chemical elements. A few minerals, such as gold and copper, are made of just one element.

- **There are over 2000** minerals, but around 30 of these are very common.

- **Most of the less common** minerals are present in rocks in minute traces. They may become concentrated in certain places by geological processes.

- **Silicate minerals** are made when metals join with oxygen and silicon. There are more silicate minerals than all the other minerals together.

- **The most common** silicates are quartz and feldspar, the most common rock-forming minerals. They are major constituents in granite and other volcanic rocks.

Quartz

Galena

Pyrite

▶ *Minerals include common substances such as rock salt and rare ones such as gold and gems.*

▶ *The rich range of colours in each layer is evidence of traces of different minerals within the rocks.*

- **Other common minerals** are oxides such as haematite and cuprite, sulphates such as gypsum and barite, sulphides such as galena and pyrite, and carbonates such as calcite and aragonite.

- **Some minerals** form as hot, molten rock from the Earth's interior, some from chemicals dissolved in liquids underground, and some are made by changes to other minerals.

Gypsum

Barite

Calcite

39

Mineral resources

- **The Earth's surface** contains an enormous wealth of mineral resources, from clay for bricks to precious gems such as rubies and diamonds.

- **Fossil fuels** are oil, coal and natural gas.

- **Fossil fuels were made** from the remains of plants and animals that lived millions of years ago. The remains were changed into fuel by intense heat and pressure.

- **Coal** is made from plants that grew in huge swamps during the Carboniferous Period 300 million years ago.

- **Oil and natural gas** were made from the remains of tiny plants and animals that lived in warm seas.

- **Ores** are the minerals from which metals are extracted. Bauxite is the ore for aluminium; chalcopyrite for copper; galena for lead; hematite for iron; sphalerite for zinc.

- **Veins** are narrow pipes of rock that are rich in minerals such as gold and silver. They are made when hot liquids made from volcanic material underground seep upwards through cracks in the rock.

▲ *Bulk materials such as cement, gravel and clay are taken from the ground in huge quantities for building.*

▲ *Strip mining is one process we use to obtain minerals from the earth. These minerals include salt, gold, diamonds, coal, gravel and iron.*

● **Mineral resources** can be located by studying rock strata (layers), often by satellite and by taking rock samples.

● **Geophysical prospecting** is hunting for minerals using physics – looking for variations in the rock's electrical conductivity, magnetism, gravity or moisture content.

● **Seismic surveys** try to locate minerals using sound vibrations, often generated by underground explosions.

41

Gems and crystals

- **Gems** are mineral crystals that are beautifully coloured or sparkling.

- **There are over 3000 minerals** but only 130 are gemstones. Only about 50 of these are commonly used.

- **The rarest gems** are called precious gems and include diamonds, emeralds and rubies.

- **Less rare gems** are known as semi-precious gems.

- **Gems** are weighed in carats. A carat is one-fifth of a gram. A 50-carat sapphire is very large and very valuable.

- **In the ancient world** gems were weighed with carob seeds. The word 'carat' comes from the Arabic for seed.

▲ *Many minerals are made as magma cools. When this happens crystals, such as amethyst crystals, are formed.*

▶ *There are more than 100 different kinds of gemstone.*

Garnet

Diamond

- **Gems** often form in gas bubbles called geodes in cooling magma. They can also form when hot magma packed with minerals seeps up through cracks in the rock to form a vein.

Topaz

- **When magma** cools, minerals with the highest melting points crystallize first. Unusual minerals are left behind to crystallize last, forming rocks called pegmatites. These rocks are often rich in gems such as emeralds, garnets, topazes and tourmalines.

- **Some gems** with a high melting point and simple chemical composition form directly from magma, such as diamond, which is pure carbon, and rubies.

Emerald

> ...FASCINATING FACT...
> Diamonds are among the oldest mineral
> crystals, over 3000 million years old.

43

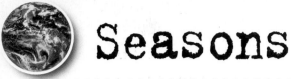

Seasons

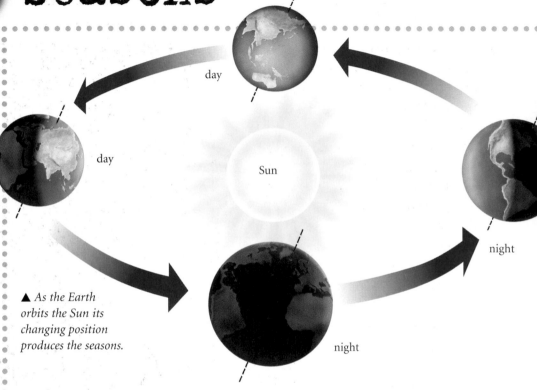

day

day

Sun

night

night

▲ *As the Earth orbits the Sun its changing position produces the seasons.*

- **Seasons** are periods in a year that bring changes in weather and temperature.

- **Outside the tropics** there are four seasons each year. Each one lasts about three months.

- **The changes in the seasons** occur because the tilt of the Earth's axis is always the same as it circles the Sun.

- **When the Earth** is on one side of the Sun, the Northern Hemisphere (half of the world) is tilted towards the Sun. It is summer in the north of the world and winter in the south.

- **As the Earth moves** a quarter way round the Sun, the northern half begins to tilt away. This brings cooler autumn weather to the north and spring to the south.

- **When the Earth** moves another quarter round to the far side of the Sun, the Northern Hemisphere is tilted away from the Sun. It is winter in the north of the world, and summer in the south.

- **As the Earth moves** three-quarters of the way round the Sun, the north begins to tilt towards the Sun again. This brings the warmer weather of spring to the north, and autumn to the south.

- **Around March 21** and September 21, the night is exactly 12 hours long all over the world. These times are called the vernal (spring) equinox and the autumnal equinox.

- **The day when** nights begin to get longer again is called the summer solstice. This is around June 21 in the north and December 21 in the south.

- **Many places** in the tropics have just two six-month seasons: wet and dry.

▲ *In autumn, the leaves of deciduous trees change colour then drop off ready for winter. Nights grow cooler, and a mist will often develop by morning.*

45

Volcanoes

- **Volcanoes** are places where magma (red-hot liquid rock from the Earth's interior) emerges through the crust and onto the surface.

- **The word 'volcano'** comes from Vulcano Island in the Mediterranean. Here Vulcan, the ancient Roman god of fire and blacksmith to the gods, was supposed to have forged his weapons in the fire beneath the mountain.

- **There are many types** of volcano (see kinds of volcano). The most distinctive are the cone-shaped composite volcanoes, which build up from alternating layers of ash and lava in successive eruptions.

- **Beneath a composite volcano** there is typically a large reservoir of magma called a magma chamber. Magma collects in the chamber before an eruption.

- **From the magma chamber** a narrow chimney, or vent, leads up to the surface. It passes through the cone of debris from previous eruptions.

- **When a volcano erupts,** the magma is driven up the vent by the gases within it. As the magma nears the surface, the pressure drops, allowing the gases dissolved in the magma to boil out. The expanding gases – mostly carbon dioxide and steam – push the molten rock upwards and out of the vent.

> **...FASCINATING FACT...**
> At Urgüp, Turkey, volcanic ash has been blown into tall cones by gas fumes bubbling up. The cones have hardened like huge salt cellars. People have dug them out to make homes.

- **If the level of magma** in the magma chamber drops, the top of the volcano's cone may collapse into it, forming a giant crater called a caldera. Caldera is Spanish for 'boiling pot'. The world's largest caldera is Toba on Sumatra, Indonesia, which is 1775 sq km.

- **When a volcano** with a caldera subsides, the whole cone may collapse into the old magma chamber. The caldera may fill with water to form a crater lake, such as Crater Lake in Oregon, USA.

- **All the magma** does not gush up the central vent. Some exits through branching side vents, often forming their own small 'parasitic' cones on the side of the main one.

Volcanic bombs, or tephra, are fragments of the shattered volcanic plug flung out far and wide

Before each eruption, the vent is clogged by old volcanic material from previous eruptions. The explosion blows the plug into tiny pieces of ash and cinder, and blasts them high into the air

Central vent

Side vent

Magma chamber where magma collects before an eruption

Lava and ash

- **When a volcano erupts** it sends out a variety of hot materials, including lava, tephra, ash and gases.

- **Lava is hot molten rock** from the Earth's interior. It is called magma while it is still underground.

- **Tephra** is material blasted into the air by an eruption. It includes pyroclasts (solid lava) and volcanic bombs.

- **Pyroclasts** are big chunks of volcanic rock that are thrown out by explosive volcanoes when the plug in the volcano's vent shatters. 'Pyroclast' means fire broken. Pyroclasts are usually 0.3 –1 m across.

- **Big eruptions** can blast pyroclasts weighing 1 tonne or more up into the air at the speed of a jet plane.

▶ *The ash hurled out from a volcano can settle and form a layer many metres deep, completely covering roads.*

- **Cinders and lapilli** are small pyroclasts. Cinders are 6.4–30 cm in diameter; lapilli are 0.1–6.4 cm.

- **Volcanic bombs** are blobs of molten magma that cool and harden in flight.

- **Breadcrust bombs** are bombs that stretch into loaf shapes in flight; gases inside them create a 'crust'.

- **Around 90% of the material** ejected by explosive volcanoes is not lava, but tephra and ash.

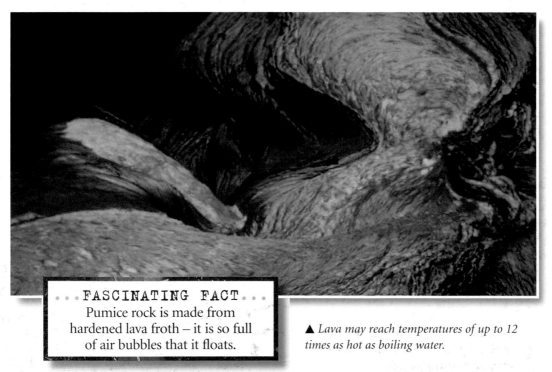

. . .FASCINATING FACT. . . .
Pumice rock is made from hardened lava froth – it is so full of air bubbles that it floats.

▲ *Lava may reach temperatures of up to 12 times as hot as boiling water.*

49

Kinds of volcano

▲ *These volcanoes are a shield volcano (top), a crater volcano (middle) and a cone-shaped volcano (bottom).*

- **Each volcano and each eruption** are slightly different.

- **Shield volcanoes** are shaped like upturned shields. They form where lava is runny and spreads over a wide area.

- **Fissure volcanoes** are found where floods of lava pour out of a long crack in the ground.

- **Composite volcanoes** are cone-shaped. They build up in layers from a succession of explosive eruptions.

- **Cinder cones** are built up from ash, with little lava.

- **Strombolian eruptions** are eruptions from sticky magma. They spit out sizzling clots of red-hot lava.

- **Vulcanian eruptions** are explosive eruptions from sticky magma. The magma clogs the volcano's vent between cannon-like blasts of ash clouds and thick lava flows.

- **Peléean eruptions** eject glowing clouds of ash and gas called nuée ardente (see famous eruptions).

- **Plinian eruptions** are the most explosive kind of eruption. They are named after Pliny who witnessed the eruption of Vesuvius in AD 79 (see famous eruptions).

- **In Plinian eruptions** boiling gases blast clouds of ash and volcanic fragments up into the stratosphere.

▲ *Fissure volcanoes shoot lava fountains in the air. This happens when gases in the lava boil suddenly as they reach the surface.*

Volcanic eruptions

- **Volcanic eruptions** are produced by magma, the hot liquid rock under the Earth's surface. Magma is less dense than the rock above, and so it tries to bubble to the surface.

- **When magma** is runny, eruptions are 'effusive', which means they ooze lava gently all the time.

- **When magma** is sticky, eruptions are explosive. The magma clogs the volcano's vent until so much pressure builds up that the magma bursts out, like a popping champagne cork.

- **The explosion** shatters the plug of hard magma that blocks the volcano's vent, reducing it to ash and cinder.

▶ *This is the eruption of Mount St Helens, USA. There are about 60 major volcanic eruptions each year around the world, including two or three huge, violent eruptions.*

... FASCINATING FACT ...
Pressure of the magma below a volcano is 10
times greater than pressure on the surface.

- **Explosive eruptions** are driven by expanding bubbles of carbon dioxide gas and steam inside the magma.

- **An explosive eruption** blasts globs of hot magma, ash, cinder, gas and steam high up into the air.

- **Volcanoes** usually erupt again and again. The interval between eruptions, called the repose time, varies from a few minutes to thousands of years.

- **Magma near subduction zones** contains 10 times more gas, so the volcanic eruptions here are violent.

- **The gas inside magma** can expand hundreds of times in just a few seconds.

▶ *Krakatau is a volcano in Indonesia. It erupted in 1883 and produced sea waves almost 40 m high, which drowned about 36,000 people.*

Volcano zones

▲ *Most volcanoes are found around the Pacific Ocean. They also occur in Iceland, Hawaii and southern Europe.*

- **Worldwide** there are over 1500 volcanoes; 500 of these are active. A volcano can have a lifespan of a million years and not erupt for several centuries.

- **Volcanoes** are said to be active if they have erupted recently. The official Smithsonian Institute list of active volcanoes includes any that have erupted in the past 10,000 years. Extinct volcanoes will never erupt again.

- **Volcanoes** occur either along the margins of tectonic plates, or over hot spots in the Earth's interior.

- **Some volcanoes** erupt where the plates are pulling apart, such as under the sea along mid-ocean ridges.

- **Some volcanoes** lie near subduction zones, forming either an arc of volcanic islands or a line of volcanoes on land, called a volcanic arc.

- **Subduction zone volcanoes** are explosive, because the magma gets contaminated and acidic as it burns up through the overlying plate. Acidic magma is sticky and gassy. It clogs up volcanic vents then blasts its way out.

- **Around the Pacific** there is a ring of explosive volcanoes called the Ring of Fire. It includes Mt Pinatubo in the Philippines, and Mt St Helens in Washington State, USA.

- **Away from subduction zones** magma is basaltic. It is runny and low in gas, so the volcanoes here gush lava.

▲ *One of many volcanoes in the Ring of Fire is Mt Rainier, in Washington State, USA.*

- **Effusive volcanoes** pour out lava frequently but gently.

- **3D radar interferometry** from satellites may pick up the minutest swelling on every active volcano in the world. In this way it helps to predict when eruptions may occur.

Hot-spot volcanoes

- **About 5% of volcanoes** are not near the margins of tectonic plates. Instead they are over especially hot places in the Earth's interior called hot spots.

- **Hot spots** are created by mantle plumes – hot currents that rise all the way from the core through the mantle.

- **When mantle plumes** come up under the crust, they burn their way through to become hot-spot volcanoes.

- **Famous hot-spot volcanoes** include the Hawaiian island volcanoes and Réunion Island in the Indian Ocean.

▲ *Hot spots pump out huge amounts of lava.*

- **Hot-spot volcanoes** ooze runny lava that spreads out to create shield volcanoes (see kinds of volcano).

- **Lava** from hot-spot volcanoes also creates plateaux, such as the Massif Central in France.

- **The geysers, hot springs and bubbling mud pots** of Yellowstone National Park, USA, indicate a hot spot below.

- **Yellowstone** has had three huge eruptions in the past 2 million years. The first produced over 2000 times as much lava as the 1980 eruption of Mt St Helens.

- **Hot spots** stay in the same place while tectonic plates slide over the top of them. Each time the plate moves, the hot spot creates a new volcano.

- **The movement** of the Pacific plate over the Hawaiian hot spot has created a chain of old volcanoes 6000 km long. It starts with the Meiji seamount under the sea north of Japan, and ends with the Hawaiian islands.

▶ *There are at least 200 geysers in Yellowstone National Park.*

Famous eruptions

▲ *The eruption of Mt St Helens in Washington, USA on May 18, 1980 blew away the side of the mountain. It sent out a blast of gas that flattened trees for 30 km around.*

● **One of the biggest- ever eruptions** occurred 2.2 million years ago in Yellowstone, USA. It poured out enough magma to build half a dozen Mt Fujiyamas.

● **In 1645 BC** the Greek island of Thera erupted, destroying the Minoan city of Akroteri. It may be the origin of the Atlantis myth.

● **On August 24, AD 79** the volcano Mt Vesuvius in Italy erupted. It buried the Roman town of Pompeii in ash.

- **The remains** of Pompeii were discovered in the 18th century, wonderfully preserved under metres of ash. They provide a remarkable snapshot of ancient Roman life.

- **The eruption** of the volcanic island of Krakatoa near Java in 1883 was heard a quarter of the way round the world.

- **In 1815** the eruption of Tambora in Indonesia was 60–80 times bigger than the 1980 eruption of Mt St Helens.

- **Ash from Tambora** filled the sky, making the summer of 1816 cool all around the world.

- **J. M. W. Turner's paintings** may have been inspired by fiery sunsets caused by dust from Tambora.

- **During the eruption of Mt Pelée** on Martinique on May 8, 1902, all but two of the 29,000 townspeople of nearby St Pierre were killed in a few minutes by a scorching flow of gas, ash and cinders.

- **The biggest eruption** in the past 50 years was that of Mt Pinatubo in the Philippines in April 1991.

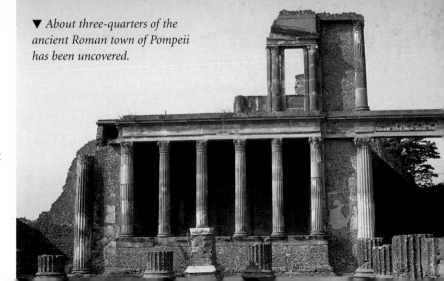

▼ *About three-quarters of the ancient Roman town of Pompeii has been uncovered.*

Earthquakes

- **Earthquakes** are a shaking of the ground. Some are slight tremors that barely rock a cradle. Others are so violent they can tear down mountains.

- **Small earthquakes** may be set off by landslides, volcanoes or even just heavy traffic. Big earthquakes are set off by the grinding together of the vast tectonic plates that make up the Earth's surface.

- **Tectonic plates** are sliding past each other all the time, but sometimes they stick. The rock bends and stretches for a while and then snaps. This makes the plates jolt, sending out the shock waves that cause the earthquake's effects to be felt far away.

- **Tectonic plates** typically slide 4 or 5 cm past each other in a year. In a slip that triggers a major quake they can slip more than 1 m in a few seconds.

- **In most quakes** a few minor tremors (foreshocks) are followed by an intense burst lasting just one or two minutes. A second series of minor tremors (aftershocks) occurs over the next few hours.

- **The starting point** of an earthquake below ground is called the hypocentre, or focus. The epicentre of an earthquake is the point on the surface directly above the hypocentre.

- **Earthquakes are strongest** at the epicentre and become gradually weaker farther away.

- **Certain regions** called earthquake zones are especially prone to earthquakes. Earthquake zones lie along the edges of tectonic plates.

- **A shallow earthquake** originates 0–70 km below the ground. These are the ones that do the most damage. An intermediate quake begins 70–300 km down. Deep quakes begin over 300 km down. The deepest-ever recorded earthquake began over 720 km down.

▼ *During an earthquake, shock waves radiate in circles outwards and upwards from the focus of the earthquake. The damage caused is greatest at the epicentre, where the waves are strongest, but vibrations may be felt 400 km away.*

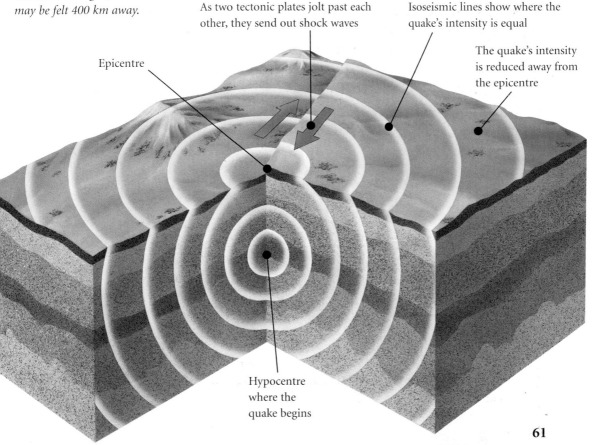

Epicentre

As two tectonic plates jolt past each other, they send out shock waves

Isoseismic lines show where the quake's intensity is equal

The quake's intensity is reduced away from the epicentre

Hypocentre where the quake begins

61

Earthquake waves

- **Earthquake waves** are the vibrations sent out through the ground by earthquakes (see earthquakes). They are also called seismic waves.

- **There are two kinds** of deep earthquake wave: primary (P) waves and secondary (S) waves.

- **P waves** travel at 5 km per second and move by alternately squeezing and stretching rock.

- **S waves** travel at 3 km per second and move the ground up and down or from side to side.

- **There are two kinds** of surface wave: Love waves and Rayleigh waves.

- **Love, or Q, waves** shake the ground from side to side in a jerky movement that can often destroy very tall buildings.

- **Rayleigh, or R, waves** shake the ground up and down, often making it seem to roll.

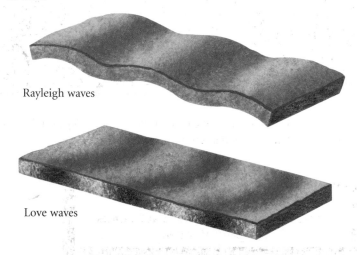

Rayleigh waves

Love waves

◄ Surface waves travel much slower than deep waves, but they are usually the ones that cause the most damage.

- **In solid ground** earthquake waves travel too fast to be seen. However, they can turn loose sediments into a fluid-like material so that earthquake waves can be seen rippling across the ground like waves in the sea.

- **When waves ripple** across loose sediment they can uproot tall buildings.

▲ *The city of Los Angeles in the USA lies on the Andreas Fault. Because of its high earthquake risk, many of its buildings are now built with reinforcements to protect against earthquake shock waves.*

> **. . . FASCINATING FACT . . .**
> Some earthquake waves travel at 20 times
> the speed of sound.

Earthquake prediction

- **One way to predict earthquakes** is to study past quakes.

- **If there has been no earthquake** in an earthquake zone for a while, there will be one soon. The longer it has been since the last quake, the bigger the next one will be.

- **Seismic gaps** are places in active earthquake zones where there has been no earthquake activity. This is where a big earthquake will probably occur.

- **Seismologists** make very accurate surveys with ground instruments and laser beams bounced off satellites (see earthquake measurement). They can spot tiny deformations of rock that show strain building up.

- **A linked network** of four laser-satellite stations called Keystone is set to track ground movements in Tokyo Bay, Japan, so that earthquakes can be predicted better.

- **The level of water** in the ground may indicate stress as the rock squeezes groundwater towards the surface. Chinese seismologists check water levels in wells.

- **Rising surface levels** of the underground gas radon may also show that the rock is being squeezed.

- **Other signs of strain** in the rock may be changes in the ground's electrical resistance or its magnetism.

- **Before an earthquake** dogs are said to howl, chickens flee their roosts, rats and mice scamper from their holes and fish thrash about in ponds.

- **Some people** claim to be sensitive to earthquakes.

◀ *Modern earthquake prediction methods detect minute distortions of the ground that indicate the rock is under stress. Seismologists use the latest survey techniques, with precision instruments like this laser rangefinder.*

▶ *Seismologists record the size of the cracks in the ground caused by earthquakes.*

65

Earthquake damage

- **Many of the world's** major cities are located in earthquake zones, such as Los Angeles, Mexico City and Tokyo.

- **Severe earthquakes** can shake down buildings and rip up flyovers.

- **When freeways collapsed** in the 1989 San Francisco quake, some cars were crushed to just 0.5 m thick.

- **The 1906 earthquake** in San Francisco destroyed 400 km of railway track around the city.

- **Some of the worst** earthquake damage is caused by fire, often set off by the breaking of gas pipes and electrical cables.

- **In 1923,** 200,000 died in the firestorm that engulfed Tokyo as an earthquake upset domestic charcoal stoves.

- **In the Kobe** earthquake of 1995 and the San Francisco earthquake of 1989 some of the worst damage was to buildings built on landfill – loose material piled in to build up the land.

▲ *The complete collapse of overhead freeways is a major danger in severe earthquakes.*

- **The earthquake** that killed the most people was probably the one that hit Shansi in China in 1556. It may have claimed 830,000 lives.

- **The most fatal** earthquake this century destroyed the city of Tangshan in China in 1976. It killed an estimated 255,000 people.

- **The worst earthquake** to hit Europe centred on Lisbon, Portugal, in 1755. It destroyed the city, killing 100,000 or more people. It probably measured 9.0 on the Richter scale (see earthquake measurement) and was felt in Paris.

▲ *Earthquakes can begin as much as 700 km below the Earth's surface. The damage they cause can be devastating, ranging from the collapse of buildings to huge cracks in the road.*

Earthquake measurement

- **Earthquakes** are measured with a device called a seismograph.

- **The Richter scale** measures the magnitude (size) of an earthquake on a scale of 1 to 10 using a seismograph. Each step in the scale indicates a tenfold increase in the energy of the earthquake.

- **The Richter scale** was devised in the 1930s by an American geophysicist called Charles Richter (1900-85).

▲ *The Richter scale tells us how much energy an earthquake has – but the damage it does to somewhere depends on how far the place is from the centre.*

- **The most powerful** earthquake ever recorded was in Chile in 1960, which registered 9.5 on the Richter scale. The 1976 Tangshan earthquake registered 7.8.

- **Between 10 and 20** earthquakes each year reach 7 on the Richter scale.

- **The Modified Mercalli scale** assesses an earthquake's severity according to its effects on a scale of 1 to 12 in Roman numerals (I–XII).

- **The Mercalli scale** was devised by the Italian scientist Guiseppe Mercalli (1850–1914).

- **A Mercalli scale I** earthquake is one that is only detectable with special instruments.

- **A Mercalli scale XII** earthquake causes almost total destruction of cities and reshapes the landscape.

- **The Moment-magnitude** scale combines Richter readings with observations of rock movements.

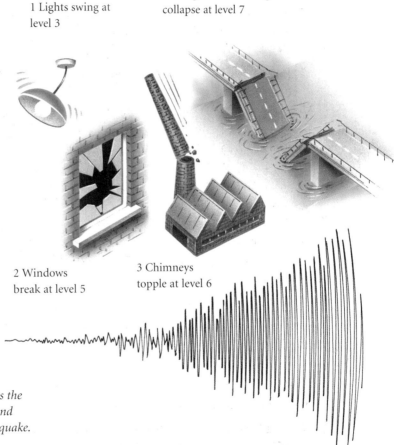

1 Lights swing at level 3

4 Bridges and buildings collapse at level 7

2 Windows break at level 5

3 Chimneys topple at level 6

▶ *The Richter scale measures the strength of the shock waves and energy produced by an earthquake.*

Famous earthquakes

- **In 1906** San Francisco, USA, was shaken by an earthquake that lasted three minutes. The earthquake started fires that burned the city almost flat.

- **The palaces** of the Minoan people on Crete were destroyed by an earthquake in about 1750 BC.

- **The earliest documented earthquake** hit the ancient Greek town of Sparta in 464 BC, killing 20,000 people.

- **In AD 62** the musical debut of the Roman Emperor Nero in Naples was ended by an earthquake.

- **In July 1201** an earthquake rocked every city in the eastern Mediterranean. It may have killed well over 1 million people.

- **In 1556** an earthquake, which is thought to have been about 8.3 on the Richter scale, hit the province of Shansi in China (see earthquake damage).

- **The 1923** earthquake which devastated Tokyo and Yokohama (see earthquake damage) also made the sea-bed in nearby Sagami Bay drop over 400 m.

- **The 1755 Lisbon earthquake** (see earthquake damage) prompted the French writer Voltaire to write *Candide*, a book that inspired the French and American revolutions.

- **The Michoacán earthquake** of 1985 killed 35,000 in Mexico City 360 km away. Silts (fine soils) under the city amplified the ground movements 75 times.

- **The 1970 earthquake** in Peru shook 50 million cubic metres of rock and ice off the peak Huascaran. They roared down at 350 km/h and swept away the town of Yungay.

▲ *The San Francisco earthquake was so strong that its effects were detected thousands of miles away. More than two-thirds of its population were left homeless.*

Rivers

- **Rivers** are filled with water from rainfall running directly off the land, from melting snow or ice or from a spring bubbling out water that is soaked into the ground.

- **High up in mountains** near their source (start), rivers are usually small. They tumble over rocks through narrow valleys which they carved out over thousands of years.

▲ *A river typically tumbles over boulders high up near its source.*

- **All the rivers** in a certain area, called a catchment area, flow down to join each other, like branches on a tree. The branches are called tributaries. The bigger the river, the more tributaries it is likely to have.

- **As rivers flow downhill,** they are joined by tributaries and grow bigger. They often flow in smooth channels made not of big rocks but of fine debris washed down from higher up. River valleys are wider and gentler lower down, and the river may wind across the valley floor.

- **In its lower reaches** a river is often wide and deep. It winds back and forth in meanders (see river channels) across broad floodplains made of silt from higher up.

- **Rivers flow fast** over rapids in their upper reaches. On average, they flow as fast in the lower reaches where the channel is smoother because there is much less turbulence.

- **Rivers wear away** their banks and beds, mainly by battering them with bits of gravel and sand and by the sheer force of the moving water.

- **Every river** carries sediment, which consists of large stones rolled along the river-bed, sand bounced along the bed and fine silt that floats in the water.

- **The discharge of a river** is the amount of water flowing past a particular point each second.

- **Rivers that flow** only after heavy rainstorms are 'intermittent'. Rivers that flow all year round are 'perennial' – they are kept going between rains by water flowing from underground.

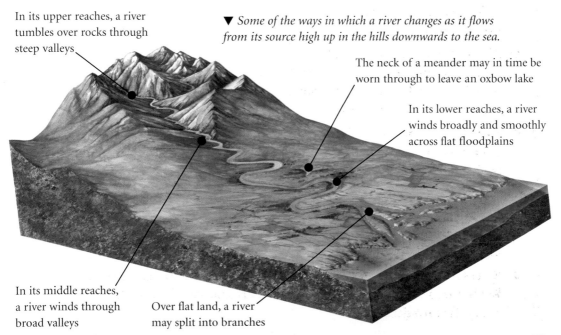

In its upper reaches, a river tumbles over rocks through steep valleys

▼ *Some of the ways in which a river changes as it flows from its source high up in the hills downwards to the sea.*

The neck of a meander may in time be worn through to leave an oxbow lake

In its lower reaches, a river winds broadly and smoothly across flat floodplains

In its middle reaches, a river winds through broad valleys

Over flat land, a river may split into branches

73

River channels

- **A channel** is the long trough along which a river flows.

- **When a river's channel** winds or has a rough bed, friction slows the river down.

- **A river flows faster** through a narrow, deep channel than a wide, shallow one because there is less friction.

- **All river channels** tend to wind, and the nearer they are to sea level, the more they wind. They form remarkably regular horseshoe-shaped bends called meanders.

- **Meanders** seem to develop because of the way in which a river erodes and deposits sediments.

▼ *River channels come to an end when they reach the mouth where the water flows into a larger river, lake or ocean.*

▲ *The river here is so wide and flat, and its bed so rough, that the water's flow is slowed by friction.*

- **One key factor** in meanders is the ups and downs along the river called pools (deeps) and riffles (shallows).

- **The distance between pools and riffles,** and the size of meanders, are in close proportion to the river's width.

- **Another key factor** in meanders is the tendency of river water to flow not only straight downstream but also across the channel. Water spirals through the channel in a corkscrew fashion called helicoidal flow.

- **Helicoidal flow** makes water flow faster on the outside of bends, wearing away the bank. It flows more slowly on the inside, building up deposits called slip-off slopes.

. . . . **FASCINATING FACT** . . . .
Meanders can form almost complete loops with only a neck of land separating the ends.

River valleys

- **Rivers** carve out valleys as they wear away their channels.

- **High up in the mountains,** much of a river's energy goes into carving into the river-bed. The valleys there are deep, with steep sides.

- **Down** towards the sea, more of a river's erosive energy goes into wearing away its banks. It carves out a broader valley as it winds back and forth.

- **Large meanders** normally develop only when a river is crossing broad plains in its lower reaches.

- **Incised meanders** are meanders carved into deep valleys. The meanders formed when the river was flowing across a low plain. The plain was lifted up and the river cut down into it, keeping its meanders.

- **The Grand Canyon** is made of incised meanders. They were created as the Colorado River cut into the Colorado Plateau after it was uplifted 17 million years ago.

- **The shape of a river valley** depends partly on the structure of the rocks over which it is flowing.

◀ *Snake-like bends in a river's course are called meanders. They are often only separated by a narrow strip of land.*

▲ *Rivers carve out valleys over hundreds of thousands of years as they grind material along their beds.*

- **Some valleys** seem far too big for their river alone to have carved them. Such a river is 'underfit', or 'misfit'.

- **Many large valleys** with misfit rivers were carved out by glaciers or glacial meltwaters.

- **The world's rivers** wear the entire land surface down by an average of 8 cm every 1000 years.

Waterfalls

▲ *About 10 million people visit Niagara Falls each year.*

● **Waterfalls** are places where a river plunges vertically.

● **Waterfalls** may form where the river flows over a band of hard rock, such as a volcanic sill. The river erodes the soft rock below but it has little effect on the hard band.

● **Waterfalls** can also form where a stream's course has been suddenly broken, for example where it flows over a cliff into the sea, over a fault (see faults) or over a hanging valley (see glaciated landscapes).

- **Boulders often swirl** around at the foot of a waterfall, wearing out a deep plunge pool.

> **·····FASCINATING FACT·····**
> The world's highest falls are the Angel Falls in Venezuela, which plunge 979 m.

- **Angel Falls** are named after American pilot Jimmy Angel who flew over them in 1935.

- **Victoria Falls** in Zimbabwe are known locally as Mosi oa Tunya, which means 'the smoke that thunders'.

- **The roar** from Victoria Falls can be heard 40 km away.

- **Niagara Falls** on the US/Canadian border developed where the Niagara River flows out of Lake Erie.

- **Niagara Falls** has two falls: Horseshoe Falls, 54 m high, and American Falls, 55 m high.

▶ *The spectacular Iguacu Falls in Brazil are made up from 275 individual falls cascading 82 m into the gorge below.*

Floods

▲ *In 1993 heavy rain over the course of two months in Mid-west America resulted in flooding causing about $12 billion worth of damage to property.*

- **A flood** is when a river or the sea rises so much that it spills over the surrounding land.

- **River floods** may occur after a period of prolonged heavy rain or after snow melts in spring.

- **Small floods** are common; big floods are rare. So flood size is described in terms of frequency.

- **A two-year flood** is a smallish flood that is likely to occur every two years. A 100-year flood is a big flood that is likely to occur once a century.

- **A flash flood** occurs when a small stream changes to a raging torrent after heavy rain during a dry spell.

- **The 1993 flood** on the Mississippi–Missouri caused damage of $15,000 million and made 75,000 homeless, despite massive flood control works in the 1930s.

- **The Hwang Ho river** is called 'China's sorrow' because its floods are so devastating.

- **Not all floods** are bad. Before the Aswan Dam was built, Egyptian farmers relied on the yearly flooding of the River Nile to enrich the soil.

- **After the Netherlands** was badly flooded by a North Sea surge in 1953, the Dutch embarked on the Delta project, one of the biggest flood control schemes in history.

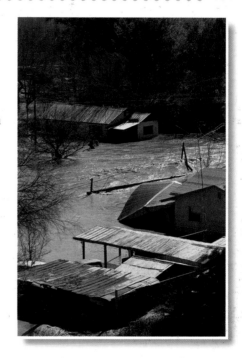

▲ *Even when no one drowns, a flood can destroy homes and wash away soil from farmland, leaving it barren.*

· · · FASCINATING FACT · · ·
In 1887, 1 million people were killed when the Hwang Ho river in China flooded.

Weathering

- **Weathering** is the gradual breakdown of rocks when they are exposed to the air.

- **Weathering affects** surface rocks the most, but water trickling into the ground can weather rocks 200 m down.

- **The more extreme** the climate, the faster weathering takes place, whether the climate is very cold or very hot.

- **In tropical Africa** the basal weathering front (the lowest limit of weathering underground) is often 60 m down.

- **Weathering** works chemically (through chemicals in rainwater), mechanically (through temperature changes) and organically (through plants and animals).

- **Chemical weathering** is when gases dissolve in rain to form weak acids that corrode rocks such as limestone.

▲ *Weathering is the breaking up of rocks by agents such as water, ice, chemicals and changing temperature.*

▶ *The desert heat means that both the chemical and the mechanical weathering of the rocks is intense.*

● **The main form of mechanical weathering** is frost shattering – when water expands as it freezes in cracks in the rocks and so shatters the rock.

● **Thermoclastis** is when desert rocks crack as they get hot and expand in the day, then cool and contract at night.

● **Exfoliation** is when rocks crack in layers as a weight of rock or ice above them is removed.

> ···FASCINATING FACT···
> At −22°C, ice can exert a pressure of 3000 kg on an area of rock the size of a postage stamp.

Limestone weathering

- **Streams and rainwater** absorb carbon dioxide gas from soil and air. It turns them into weak carbonic acid.

- **Carbonic acid** corrodes (wears away by dissolving) limestone in a process called carbonation.

- **When limestone rock** is close to the surface, carbonation can create spectacular scenery.

- **Corroded limestone scenery** is often called karst, because the best example of it is the Karst Plateau near Dalmatia, in Bosnia.

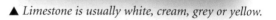

▲ *Limestone is usually white, cream, grey or yellow.*

- **On the surface,** carbonation eats away along cracks to create pavements, with slabs called clints. The slabs are separated by deeply etched grooves called grykes.

- **Limestone rock** does not soak up water like a sponge. It has massive cracks called joints, and streams and rainwater trickle deep into the rock through these cracks.

- **Streams** drop down into limestone through swallow-holes, like bathwater down a plughole. Carbonation eats out such holes to form giant shafts called potholes.

- **Some potholes** are eaten out to create great funnel-shaped hollows called dolines, up to 100 m across.

- **Where water** streams out along horizontal cracks at the base of potholes, the rock may be etched out into caverns.

- **Caverns** may be eaten out so much that the roof collapses to form a gorge or a large hole called a polje.

▲ *Corrosion by underground streams in limestone can eat out huge caverns, often filled with spectacular stalactites and stalagmites (see caves).*

Caves

▲ *Caverns can be subterranean palaces filled with glistening pillars.*

● **Caves** are giant holes that run horizontally underground. Holes that plunge vertically are called potholes.

● **The most spectacular caves,** called caverns, are found in limestone. Acid rainwater trickles through cracks in the rock and wears away huge cavities.

● **The world's largest known** single cave is the Sarawak Chamber in Gunung Mulu in Sarawak, Malaysia.

● **The deepest** cave gallery yet found is the Pierre St Martin system, 800 m down in the French Pyrenees.

- **The longest** cave system is the Mammoth Cave in Kentucky, USA, which is 560 km long.

- **Many caverns** contain fantastic deposits called speleothems. They are made mainly from calcium carbonate deposited by water trickling through the cave.

- **Stalactites** are icicle-like speleothems that hang from cave ceilings. Stalagmites poke upwards from the floor.

- **The world's longest** stalactite is 6.2 m long. It is in the Poll an Ionain in County Clare, Ireland.

- **The world's tallest column** is the Flying Dragon Pillar in the Nine Dragons Cave, Guizhou, China.

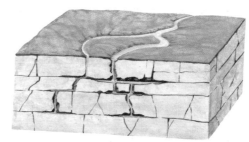

▲ Surface water flows into layers of limestone and hollows out caves.

> .....FASCINATING FACT.....
> The Sarawak Chamber is big enough to hold
> the world's biggest sports stadium 3 times over.

Ice Ages

- **Ice Ages** are periods lasting millions of years when the Earth is so cold that the polar ice caps grow huge. There are various theories about why they occur (see climate change).

- **There have been four Ice Ages** in the last 1000 million years, including one which lasted 100 million years.

- **The most recent Ice Age** – called the Pleistocene Ice Age – began about 2 million years ago.

- **In an Ice Age** the weather varies between cold spells called glacials and warm spells called interglacials.

- **There were** 17 glacials and interglacials in the last 1.6 million years of the Pleistocene Ice Age.

▶ *The people of the Ice Age risked their lives to hunt the fierce woolly mammoth. It was a good source of meat, skins, bones and ivory.*

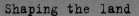

▲ California may have looked something like this 18,000 years ago when it was on the fringes of an ice sheet.

... **FASCINATING FACT** ...
Where Washington and London are today, the ice was 1.5 km thick 18,000 years ago.

- **The last glacial,** called the Holocene glacial, peaked about 18,000 years ago and ended 10,000 years ago.

- **Ice covered 40% of the world** 18,000 years ago.

- **Glaciers spread** over much of Europe and North America 18,000 years ago. Ice caps grew in Tasmania and New Zealand.

- **About 18,000 years ago** there were glaciers in Hawaii.

Icebergs

▲ *On April 14 1912 the* Titanic, *the largest passenger ship of the time, struck an iceberg and sank.*

- **Icebergs** are big lumps of floating ice that calve, or break off, from the end of glaciers or polar ice caps. This often occurs when tides and waves move the ice up and down.

- **Calving of icebergs occurs** mostly during the summer when the warm conditions partially melt the ice.

- **Around 15,000 icebergs a year** calve in the Arctic.

- **Arctic icebergs** vary from car-sized ones called growlers to mansion-sized blocks. The biggest iceberg, 11 km long, was spotted off Baffin Island in 1882.

- **The Petterman and Jungersen** glaciers in northern Greenland form big table-shaped icebergs called ice islands. They are like the icebergs found in Antarctica.

- **Antarctic icebergs** are much, much bigger than Arctic ones. The biggest iceberg, which was 300 km long, was spotted in 1956 by the icebreaker USS *Glacier*.

- **Antarctic icebergs** last for ten years on average; Arctic icebergs last for about two years.

- **The ice** that makes Arctic icebergs is 3000 - 6000 years old.

- **Each year 375 or so icebergs** drift from Greenland into the shipping lanes off Newfoundland. They are a major hazard to shipping in that area.

- **The International Ice Patrol** was set up in 1914 to monitor icebergs after the great liner Titanic sank. The liner hit an iceberg off Newfoundland in 1912.

▼ *Icebergs are big chunks of floating ice that break off glaciers.*

Glaciers

- **Glaciers** are rivers of slowly moving ice. They form in mountain regions when it is too cold for snow to melt. They flow down through valleys, creeping lower until they melt in the warm air lower down.

- **Glaciers** form when new snow, or névé, falls on top of old snow. The weight of the new snow compacts the old snow into denser snow called firn.

▲ *The dense ice in glaciers is made from thousands of years of snow. As new snow fell, the old snow beneath it became squeezed more and more in a process called firnification.*

- **In firn snow,** all the air is squeezed out so it looks like ice. As more snow falls, firn gets more compacted and becomes glacier ice flowing slowly downhill.

- **Nowadays** glaciers form only in high mountains and towards the North and South Poles. In the Ice Ages glaciers were widespread and left glaciated landscapes in many places that are now free of ice.

- **As glaciers** move downhill, they bend and stretch, opening up deep cracks called crevasses. Sometimes these occur where the glacier passes over a ridge.

- **The biggest crevasse** is often called the bergschrund. It forms when the ice pulls away from the back wall of the hollow where the glacier starts.

- **Where the underside** of a glacier is warmish (about 0°C), it moves by gliding over a film of water that is made as pressure melts the glacier's base. It is called basal slip.

- **Where the underside** of a glacier is coldish (well below 0°C), it moves as if layers were slipping over each other like a pack of cards. This is called internal deformation.

- **Valley glaciers** are glaciers that flow in existing valleys.
- **Cirque glaciers** are small glaciers that flow from hollows high up. Alpine valley glaciers form when several cirque glaciers merge. Piedmont glaciers form where valley glaciers join as they emerge from the mountains.

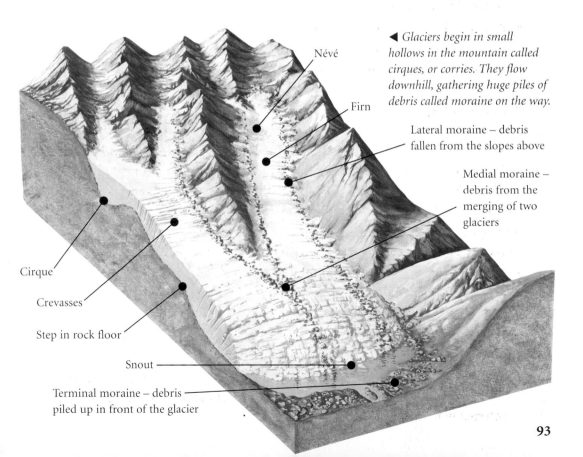

Névé

Firn

◀ *Glaciers begin in small hollows in the mountain called cirques, or corries. They flow downhill, gathering huge piles of debris called moraine on the way.*

Lateral moraine – debris fallen from the slopes above

Medial moraine – debris from the merging of two glaciers

Cirque

Crevasses

Step in rock floor

Snout

Terminal moraine – debris piled up in front of the glacier

93

Glaciated landscapes

- **Glaciers** move slowly but their sheer weight and size give them enormous power to shape the landscape.

- **Over tens of thousands of years** glaciers carve out winding valleys into huge, straight U-shaped troughs.

- **Glaciers** may truncate (slice off) tributary valleys to leave them 'hanging', with a cliff edge high above the main valley. Hill spurs (ends of hills) may also be truncated.

▼ *Valley glaciers are long, narrow bodies of ice that fill high mountain valleys.*

▼ *After an Ice Age, glaciers leave behind a dramatically altered landscape of deep valleys and piles of debris.*

- **Cirques, or corries,** are armchair-shaped hollows carved out where a glacier begins high up in the mountains.

- **Arêtes** are knife-edge ridges that are left between several cirques as the glaciers in them cut backwards.

- **Drift** is a blanket of debris deposited by glaciers. Glaciofluvial drift is left by the water made as the ice melts. Till is left by the ice itself.

- **Drumlins** are egg-shaped mounds of till. Eskers are snaking ridges of drift left by streams under the ice.

- **Moraine** is piles of debris left by glaciers.

- **Proglacial lakes** are lakes of glacial meltwater dammed up by moraine.

...FASCINATING FACT...
After the last Ice Age, water from the huge Lake Agassiz submerged over 500,000 sq km of land near Winnipeg, in Canada.

Cold landscapes

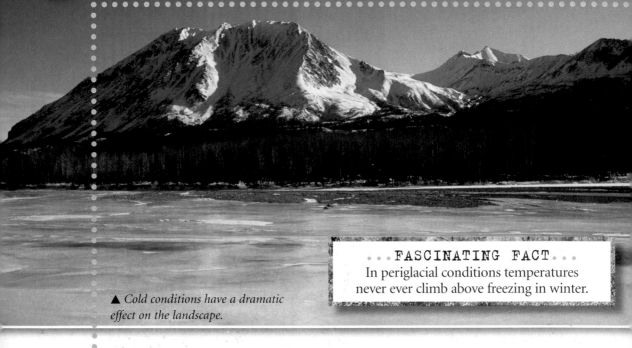

▲ *Cold conditions have a dramatic effect on the landscape.*

- **'Periglacial'** used to describe conditions next to the ice in the Ice Ages. It now means similar conditions found today.

- **Periglacial conditions** are found on the tundra of northern Canada and Siberia and on nunataks, which are the hills that protrude above ice sheets and glaciers.

- **In periglacial areas** ice only melts in spring at the surface. Deep down under the ground it remains permanently frozen permafrost.

- **When the ground** above the permafrost melts, the soil twists into buckled layers called involutions.

- **When frozen soil melts** it becomes so fluid that it can creep easily down slopes, creating large tongues and terraces.

- **Frost heave** is the process when frost pushes stones to the surface as the ground freezes.

- **After frost heave**, large stones roll down leaving the fine stones on top. This creates intricate patterns on the ground.

- **On flat ground,** quilt-like patterns are called stone polygons. On slopes, they stretch into stone stripes.

- **Pingos** are mounds of soil with a core of ice. They are created when groundwater freezes beneath a lake.

▲ *Moose become vulnerable in winter when wolves can follow them across the ice.*

97

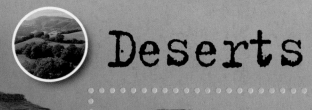

Deserts

▲ *Water erosion over millions of years has created these dramatic pillar-like mesas and buttes in Monument Valley in Utah, USA.*

- **Deserts are places** where it rarely rains. Many are hot, but one of the biggest deserts is Antarctica. Deserts cover about one-fifth of the Earth's land.

- **Hamada** is desert that is strewn with boulders. Reg is desert that is blanketed with gravel.

- **About one-fifth** of all deserts are seas of sand dunes. These are known as ergs in the Sahara.

- **The type of sand dune** depends on how much sand there is, and how changeable the wind is.

- **Barchans** are moving, crescent-shaped dunes that form in sparse sand where the wind direction is constant.

- **Seifs** are long dunes that form where sand is sparse and the wind comes from two or more directions.

- **Most streams** in deserts flow only occasionally, leaving dry stream beds called wadis or arroyos. These may suddenly fill with a flash flood after rain.

- **In cool, wet regions,** hills are covered in soil and rounded in shape. In deserts, hills are bare rock with cliff faces footed by straight slopes.

- **Mesas and buttes** are pillar-like plateaux that have been carved gradually by water in deserts.

> ...**FASCINATING FACT**...
> In the western Sahara, 2 million dry years have created sand ridges over 300 m high.

▼ *Oases are places in the desert that have water supplies. Plants and animals can thrive in these areas.*

Swamps and marshes

▲ *Swamps are home to a variety of wildlife including fish, frogs, snakes, alligators and crocodiles.*

- **Wetlands** are areas of land where the water level is mostly above the ground.

- **The main types** of wetland are bogs, fens, swamps and marshes.

- **Bogs and fens** occur in cold climates and contain plenty of partially rotted plant material called peat.

- **Marshes and swamps** are found in warm and cold places. They have more plants than bogs and fens.

- **Marshes** are in permanently wet places, such as shallow lakes and river deltas. Reeds and rushes grow in marshes.

- **Swamps** develop where the water level varies – often along the edges of rivers in the tropics where they are flooded, notably along the Amazon and Congo Rivers. Trees such as mangroves grow in swamps.

- **Half the wetlands** in the USA were drained before most people appreciated their value. Almost half of Dismal Swamp in North Carolina has been drained.

- **The Pripet Marshes** on the borders of Belorussia are the biggest in Europe, covering 270,000 sq km.

- **Wetlands act** like sponges and help to control floods.

- **Wetlands help** to top up supplies of groundwater.

▶ *In the past, wetlands were seen simply as dead areas, ripe for draining. Now their value for both wildlife and water control is beginning to be realized.*

Hills

▲ *A hill is an elevation of the Earth's surface with a distinct summit.*

- **One definition** of a hill is high ground up to 307 m high. Above that height it is a mountain.

- **Mountains are solid rock;** hills can be solid rock or piles of debris built up by glaciers or the wind.

- **Hills that are solid rock** are either very old, having been worn down from mountains over millions of years, or they are made from soft sediments that were low hills.

- **In moist climates** hills are often rounded by weathering and by water running over the land.

- **As solid rock is weathered,** the hill is covered in a layer of debris called regolith. This material either creeps slowly downhill or slumps suddenly in landslides.

▼ *The contours of hills in damp places have often been gently rounded over long periods by a combination of weathering and erosion by running water.*

- **Hills** often have a shallow S-shaped slope. Geologists call this kind of slope 'convexo-concave' because there is a short rounded convex section at the top, and a long dish-shaped concave slope lower down.

- **Hill slopes** become gentler as they are worn away, because the top is worn away faster. This is called decline.

- **Retreat is where** hill slopes stay equally steep, but are simply worn back.

- **Replacement is where** hill slopes wear back, with gentler sections becoming longer and steeper sections shorter.

- **Decline** may take place in damp places; retreat happens in dry places.

103

Changing landscapes

▲ *The Moon has no air, wind or water so the landscape changes very little.*

● **The Moon's landscape** has barely changed over billions of years. The footprints left by Moon astronauts 30 years ago are still there, perfectly preserved in dust.

● **The Earth's surface** changes all the time. Most changes take millions of years. Sometimes the landscape is reshaped suddenly by an avalanche or a volcano.

- **The Earth's surface** is distorted and re-formed from below by the huge forces of the Earth's interior.

- **The Earth's surface** is moulded from above by weather, water, waves, ice, wind and other 'agents of erosion'.

- **Most landscapes,** except deserts, are moulded by running water, which explains why hills have rounded slopes. Dry landscapes are more angular, but even in deserts water often plays a major shaping role.

- **Mountain peaks** are jagged because it is so cold high up that the rocks are often shattered by frost.

- **An American scientist** W. M. Davis (1850–1935) thought landscapes are shaped by repeated 'cycles of erosion'.

- **Davis's cycles of erosion** have three stage: vigorous 'youth', steady 'maturity' and sluggish 'old age'.

- **Observation** has shown that erosion does not become more sluggish as time goes on, as Davis believed.

- **Many landscapes** have been shaped by forces no longer in operation, such as moving ice during past Ice Ages.

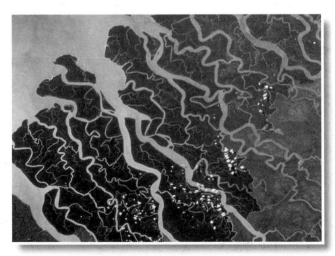

▶ *Rivers are one of the most powerful agents of erosion.*

Climate

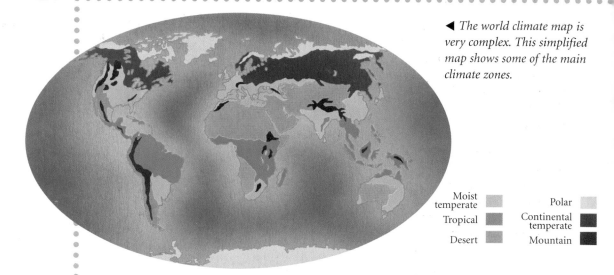

◀ *The world climate map is very complex. This simplified map shows some of the main climate zones.*

Moist temperate	Polar
Tropical	Continental temperate
Desert	Mountain

- **Climate is the typical weather** of a place over a long time.

- **Climates are warm** near the Equator, where the Sun climbs high in the sky.

- **Tropical climates** are warm climates in the tropical zones on either side of the Equator. Average temperatures of 27°C are typical.

- **The climate is cool** near the Poles, where the Sun never climbs high in the sky. Average temperatures of –30°C are typical.

- **Temperate climates** are mild climates in the temperate zones between the tropics and the polar regions. Summer temperatures may average 23°C. Winter temperatures may average 12°C.

- **A Mediterranean climate** is a temperate climate with warm summers and mild winters. It is typical of the Mediterranean, California, South Africa and South Australia.

106

▶ *The big seasonal difference in temperature is due to the movement of the overhead Sun. The polar regions are too far away from the Equator for the Sun ever to be overhead, or for there to be much seasonal difference in temperature.*

▶ *When the Mediterranean is nearest the Sun in midsummer it is hottest and driest. The coolest time of year comes when the Sun is farthest away from the Mediterranean, and closer to the southern hemisphere.*

▶ *There is little seasonal variation in temperature near the Equator. Moving away from the Equator, there are seasons. The Sun is directly above the Equator during March and September, and above the Tropics of Cancer and Capricorn in June and December.*

- **A monsoon climate** is a climate with one very wet and one very dry season – typical of India and SE Asia.

- **An oceanic climate** is a wetter climate near oceans, with cooler summers and warmer winters.

- **A continental climate** is a drier climate in the centre of continents, with hot summers and cold winters.

- **Mountain climates** get colder and windier with height.

107

Climate change

▲ *Tree rings can be used to tell what the weather has been like in the past. In wet periods the rings are thick and in dry periods the rings are thin.*

- **The world's climate** is changing all the time, getting warmer, colder, wetter or drier. There are many theories why this happens.

- **One way to see** how climate changed before weather records were kept is to look at the growth rings in old trees.

- **Another way** of working out past climate is to look in ancient sediments for remains of plants and animals that only thrive in certain conditions.

- **One cause of climate change** may be shifts in the Earth's orientation to the Sun. These shifts are called Milankovitch cycles.

- **One Milankovitch cycle** is the way the Earth's axis wobbles round like a top every 21,000 years. Another is the way its axis tilts like a rolling ship every 40,000 years. A third is the way its orbit gets more or less oval shaped every 96,000 years.

- **Climate** may also be affected by dark patches on the Sun called sunspots. These flare up and down every 11 years.

- **Sunspot activity** is linked to stormy weather on the Earth.

- **Climates may cool** when the air is filled with dust from volcanic eruptions or meteors hitting the Earth.

- **Climates** may get warmer when levels of certain gases in the air increase (see global warming).

- **Local climates** may change as continents drift around. Antarctica was once in the tropics, while the New York area once had a tropical desert climate.

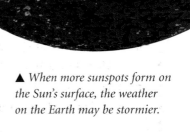

▲ *When more sunspots form on the Sun's surface, the weather on the Earth may be stormier.*

109

Atmosphere

- **The atmosphere** is a blanket of gases about 1000 km deep around the Earth. It can be divided into five layers: troposphere (the lowest), stratosphere, mesosphere, thermosphere and exosphere.

- **The atmosphere** is: 78% nitrogen, 21% oxygen, 1% argon and carbon dioxide with tiny traces of neon, krypton, zenon, helium, nitrous oxide, methane and carbon monoxide.

- **The atmosphere** was first created by the fumes pouring out from the volcanoes that covered the early Earth 4000 million years ago. But it was changed as rocks and seawater absorbed carbon dioxide, and then algae in the sea built up oxygen levels over millions and millions of years.

- **The troposphere** is just 12 km thick yet it contains 75% of the weight of gases in the atmosphere. Temperatures drop with height from 18°C on average to about –60°C at the top, called the tropopause.

- **The stratosphere** contains little water. Unlike the troposphere, which is heated from below, it is heated from above as the ozone in it is heated by ultraviolet light from the Sun. Temperatures rise with height from –60°C to 10°C at the top, about 50 km up.

- **The stratosphere** is completely clear and calm, which is why jet airliners try to fly in this layer.

- **The mesosphere** contains few gases but it is thick enough to slow down meteorites. They burn up as they hurtle into it, leaving fiery trails in the night sky. Temperatures drop from 10°C to –120°C 80 km up.

> ...**FASCINATING FACT**...
> The stratosphere glows faintly at night because sodium from salty sea spray reacts chemically in the air.

Light gases such as hydrogen and helium continually drift into space from the outer fringes of the atmosphere

Low-level satellites orbit within the outer layers of the atmosphere

Exosphere

Shimmering curtains of light called auroras appear above the poles. They are caused by the impact of particles from the Sun on the gases in the upper atmosphere

The atmosphere protects us from meteorites and radiation from space

700 km

- **In the thermosphere** temperatures are very high, but there is so little gas that there is little real heat. Temperatures rise from −120°C to 2000°C 700 km up.

Thermosphere

Mesosphere

- **The exosphere** is the highest level of the atmosphere where it fades into the nothingness of space.

The stratosphere contains the ozone layer, which protects us from the Sun's UV rays

Airliners climb to the stratosphere to find calm air

Stratosphere

The troposphere is the layer we live in

80 km: the mesopause

50 km: the stratopause

12 km: the tropopause

◄ The atmosphere is a sea of colourless, tasteless, odourless gases, mixed with moisture and fine dust particles. It is about 1000 km deep but has no distinct edge, simply fading away into space. As you move up, each layer contains less and less gas. The topmost layers are very rarefied, which means that gas is very sparse.

111

Air moisture

▲ *Clouds are the visible, liquid part of the moisture in the air. They form when the water vapour in the air cools and condenses.*

- **Up to 10 km** above the ground, the air is always moist because it contains an invisible gas called water vapour.

- **There is enough water vapour** in the air to flood the entire globe to a depth of 2.5 m.

- **Water vapour** enters the air when it evaporates from oceans, rivers and lakes.

- **Water vapour** leaves the air when it cools and condenses (turns to drops of water) to form clouds. Most clouds eventually turn to rain, and so the water falls back to the ground. This is called precipitation.

- **Like a sponge,** the air soaks up evaporating water until it is saturated (full). It can only take in more water if it warms up and expands.

- **If saturated air cools,** it contracts and squeezes out the water vapour, forcing it to condense into drops of water. The point at which this happens is called the dew point.

- **Humidity** is the amount of water in the air.

- **Absolute humidity** is the weight of water in grams in a particular volume of air.

- **Relative humidity,** which is written as a percentage, is the amount of water in the air compared to the amount of water the air could hold when saturated.

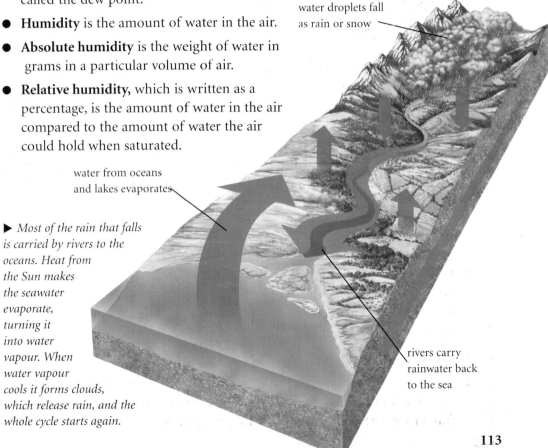

water droplets fall as rain or snow

water from oceans and lakes evaporates

▶ *Most of the rain that falls is carried by rivers to the oceans. Heat from the Sun makes the seawater evaporate, turning it into water vapour. When water vapour cools it forms clouds, which release rain, and the whole cycle starts again.*

rivers carry rainwater back to the sea

113

Clouds

▲ *Cirrus clouds appear high in the sky, sometimes at heights of over 10,000 m.*

- **Clouds are** dense masses of water drops and ice crystals that are so tiny they float high in the air.

- **Cumulus clouds** are fluffy white clouds. They pile up as warm air rises and cool to the point where water vapour condenses.

- **Strong updraughts** create huge cumulonimbus, or thunder, clouds.

▶ *Cumulus clouds build up in fluffy piles as warm, moist air rises. Once it reaches about 2000 m, the air cools enough for clouds to form.*

- **Stratus clouds** are vast shapeless clouds that form when a layer of air cools to the point where moisture condenses. They often bring long periods of light rain.

- **Cirrus clouds** are wispy clouds that form so high up they are made entirely of ice. Strong winds high up blow them into 'mares tails'.

- **Low clouds** lie below 2000 m above the ground. They include stratus and stratocumulus clouds (the spread tops of cumulus clouds).

- **Middle clouds** often have the prefix 'alto' and lie from 2000 m to 6000 m up. They include rolls of altocumulus cloud, and thin sheets called altostratus.

- **High-level clouds** are ice clouds up to 11,000 m up. They include cirrus, cirrostratus and cirrocumulus.

- **Contrails** are trails of ice crystals left by jet aircraft.

Fog and mist

▲ *Fog spreads slowly upwards from the surface of the water seen here over the Ganges in India.*

- **Like clouds,** mist is billions of tiny water droplets floating on the air. Fog forms near the ground.

- **Mist forms** when the air cools to the point where the water vapour it contains condenses to water.

- **Meteorologists** define fog as a mist that reduces visibility to less than 1 km.

- **There are four main kinds** of fog: radiation fog, advection fog, frontal fog and upslope fog.

- **Radiation fog** forms on cold, clear, calm nights. The ground loses heat that it absorbed during the day, and so cools the air above.

▲ *Huge amounts of moisture transpire from the leaves of forest trees. It condenses on cool nights to form a thick morning mist.*

- **Advection fog** forms when warm, moist air flows over a cold surface. This cools the air so much that the moisture it contains condenses.

- **Sea fog** is advection fog that forms as warm air flows out over cool coastal waters and lakes.

- **Frontal fog** forms along fronts (see weather fronts).

- **Upslope fog** forms when warm, moist air rises up a mountain and cools.

117

Rain

▲ *Rain starts when moist air is lifted up dramatically. Water drops and ice crystals inside the cloud grow so big that it turns dark.*

- **Rain falls** from clouds filled with large water drops and ice crystals. The thick clouds block out the sunlight.

- **The technical name** for rain is precipitation, which also includes snow, sleet and hail.

- **Drizzle** is 0.2–0.5 mm drops falling from nimbostratus clouds. Rain from nimbostratus is 1–2 mm drops. Drops from thunderclouds can be 5 mm. Snow is ice crystals. Sleet is a mix of rain or snow, or partly melted snow.

- **Rain starts** when water drops or ice crystals inside clouds grow too large for the air to support them.

- **Cloud drops grow** when moist air is swept upwards and cools, causing lots of drops to condense. This happens when pockets of warm, rising air form thunderclouds – at weather fronts or when air is forced up over hills.

- **In the tropics** raindrops grow in clouds by colliding with each other. In cool places, they also grow on ice crystals.

- **The world's rainiest place** is Mt Wai-'ale-'ale in Hawaii, where it rains 350 days a year.

- **The wettest place** is Tutunendo in Colombia, which gets 11,770 mm of rain every year. (London gets about 70 mm.)

- **La Réunion in the Indian Ocean** received 1870 mm of rain in one day in 1952.

- **Guadeloupe in the West Indies** received 38.1 mm of rain in one minute in 1970.

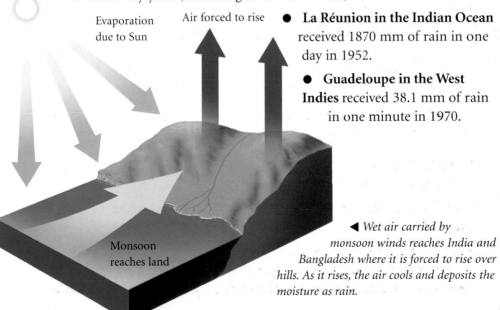

Evaporation due to Sun

Air forced to rise

Monsoon reaches land

◀ *Wet air carried by monsoon winds reaches India and Bangladesh where it is forced to rise over hills. As it rises, the air cools and deposits the moisture as rain.*

119

Thunderstorms

▲ *Large, towering cumulonimbus storm clouds can tower up to 16 km in the air.*

- **Thunderstorms** begin when strong updraughts build up towering cumulonimbus clouds.

- **Water drops** and ice crystals in thunderclouds are buffeted together. They become charged with static electricity.

- **Negative charges** sink to the base of a cloud; positive ones rise. When the different charges meet they create lightning.

- **Sheet lightning** is a flash within a cloud. Forked lightning flashes from a cloud to the ground.

- **Forked lightning** begins with a fast, dim flash from a cloud to the ground, called the leader stroke. It prepares the air for a huge, slower return stroke a split second later.

- **Thunder is the sound** of the shock wave as air expands when heated instantly to 25,000°C by the lightning.

- **Sound travels** more slowly than light, so we hear thunder three seconds later for every 1 km between us and the storm.

- **At any moment** there are 2000 thunderstorms around the world, each generating the energy of a hydrogen bomb. Every second, 100 lightning bolts hit the ground.

- **A flash of lightning** is brighter than 10 million 100-watt light bulbs. For a split second it has more power than all the power stations in the USA put together. Lightning travels at up to 100,000 km per second down a path that is the width of a finger but up to 14 km long. Sheet lightning can be 140 km long.

- **Lightning** can fuse sand under the ground into hard strands called fulgurites.

▲ *Few places have more spectacular lightning displays than Nevada, USA. The energy in clouds piled up during hot afternoons is unleashed at night.*

121

Sunshine

▲ *Without sunshine, the Earth would be cold, dark and dead.*

● **Half of the Earth** is exposed to the Sun at any time. Radiation from the Sun is the Earth's main source of energy. This provides huge amounts of both heat and light, without which there would be no life on Earth.

● **Solar** means anything to do with the Sun.

● **About 41% of solar radiation** is light; 51% is long-wave radiation that our eyes cannot see, such as infrared light. The other 8% is short-wave radiation, such as UV rays.

● **Only 47%** of the solar radiation that strikes the Earth actually reaches the ground; the rest is soaked up or reflected by the atmosphere.

- **The air is not warmed** much by the Sun directly. Instead, it is warmed by heat reflected from the ground.

- **Solar radiation** reaching the ground is called insolation.

- **The amount of heat reaching** the ground depends on the angle of the Sun's rays. The lower the Sun is in the sky, the more its rays are spread out and therefore give off less heat.

- **Insolation is at a peak** in the tropics and during the summer. It is lowest near the Poles and in winter.

- **The tropics** receive almost two and a half times more heat per day than either the North or South Pole.

- **Some surfaces** reflect the Sun's heat and warm the air better than others. The percentage they reflect is called the albedo. Snow and ice have an albedo of 85–95% and so they stay frozen even as they warm the air. Forests have an albedo of 12%, so they soak up a lot of the Sun's heat.

◀ The Sun can be used to generate electricity. When the sun shines on solar cells, electric current flows from one side of the cell to the other.

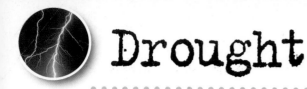

Drought

▲ *In times of drought crops, plants and animals all suffer.*

- **A drought** is a long period when there is too little rain.

- **During a drought** the soil dries out, groundwater sinks, streams stop flowing and plants die.

- **Deserts** suffer from permanent drought. Many tropical places have a seasonal drought, with long dry seasons.

- **Droughts** are often accompanied by high temperatures, which increase water loss through evaporation.

- **Between 1931 and 1938** drought reduced the Great Plains of the USA to a dustbowl, as the soil dried out and turned to dust. Drought came again from 1950 to 1954.

- **Desertification** is the spread of desert conditions into surrounding grassland. It is caused either by climate changes or by pressure from human activities.

- **Drought,** combined with increased numbers of livestock and people, have put pressure on the Sahel, south of the Sahara in Africa, causing widespread desertification.

- **Drought** has brought repeated famine to the Sahel, especially the Sudan and Ethiopia.

- **Drought** in the Sahel may be partly triggered off by El Niño – a reversal of the ocean currents in the Pacific Ocean, off Peru, which happens every 2–7 years.

- **The Great Drought** of 1276–99 destroyed the cities of the ancient Indian civilizations of southwest USA. It led to the cities being abandoned.

▲ *Drought bakes the soil so hard it shrinks and cracks. It will no longer absorb water even when rain comes.*

Cold

▲*When it is very cold, snow remains loose and powdery and is often whipped up by the wind.*

- **Winter weather is cold** because days are too short to give much heat. The Sun always rakes across the ground at a low angle, spreading out its warmth.

- **The coldest places** in the world are the North and South Poles. Here the Sun shines at a low angle even in summer, and winter nights last almost 24 hrs.

- **The average temperature** at Polus Nedostupnosti (Pole of Cold) in Antarctica is −58°C.

- **The coldest temperature** ever recorded was −89.2°C at Vostok in Antarctica on July 21, 1983.

- **The interiors of the continents** can get very cold in winter because land loses heat rapidly.

- **When air cools** below freezing point (0°C), water vapour in the air may freeze without turning first to dew. It covers the ground with white crystals of ice or frost.

- **Fern frost** is feathery tails of ice that form on cold glass as dew drops freeze bit by bit.

- **Hoar frost** is spiky needles of frost that form when damp air blows over very cold surfaces and freezes onto them.

- **Rime** is a thick coating of ice that forms when drops of water in clouds and fogs stay liquid well below freezing point. The drops freeze hard when they touch a surface.

- **Black ice** forms when rain falls on a very cold road.

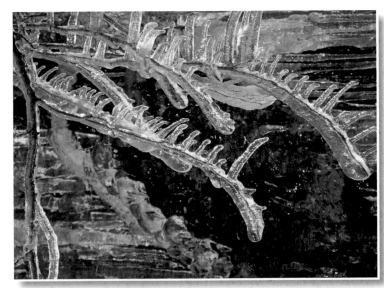

▶ *Rime is a thick coating of ice that forms when moisture cools well below 0°C, before freezing onto surfaces.*

127

Snow

- **Snow** is crystals of ice. They fall from clouds in cold weather when the air is too cold to melt ice into rain.

- **Outside the tropics** most rain starts to fall as snow but melts on the way down.

- **More snow falls** in the northern USA than falls at the North Pole because it is too cold to snow at the North Pole.

- **The heaviest** snow falls when the air temperature is hovering around freezing.

- **Snow can be hard to forecast** because a rise in temperature of just 1°C or so can turn snow into rain.

- **All snowflakes** have six sides. They usually consist of crystals that are flat plates, but occasionally needles and columns are also found.

▲ *Fresh snow can contain up to 90% air, which is why snow can actually insulate the ground and keep it warm, protecting plants.*

- **W. A. Bentley** was an American farmer who photographed thousands of snowflakes through microscopes. He never found two identical flakes.

- **In February 1959** the Mt Shaska Ski Bowl in California had 4800 mm of snow in just six days.

- **In March 1911** Tamarac in California was buried in 11,460 mm of snow. The Antarctic is buried in over 4000 m of snow.

- **The snowline** is the lowest level on a mountain where snow remains throughout the summer. It is 5000 m in the tropics, 2700 m in the Alps, 600 m in Greenland and at sea level at the Poles.

▶ *Snow is often slow to melt after it has covered the ground. This is because it reflects away the majority of the sunlight.*

Wind

- **Wind is moving air.** Strong winds are fast-moving air; gentle breezes are air that moves slowly.

- **Air moves** because the Sun warms some places more than others, creating differences in air pressure.

- **Warmth makes** air expand and rise, lowering air pressure. Cold makes air heavier, raising pressure.

- **Winds blow** from areas of high pressure to areas of low pressure, which are called lows.

- **The sharper the pressure difference** the stronger the winds blow.

▼ *Energy from the wind is converted to electricity by wind turbines.*

- **In the Northern Hemisphere,** winds spiral in a clockwise direction out of highs, and anticlockwise into lows. In the Southern Hemisphere, the reverse is true.

- **A prevailing wind** is a wind that blows frequently from the same direction. Winds are named by the direction they blow from. For instance a westerly wind blows from the west.

- **In the tropics** the prevailing winds are warm, dry winds. They blow from the northeast and the southeast towards the Equator.

- **In the mid-latitudes** the prevailing winds are warm, moist westerlies.

▲ *The more of the Sun's energy there is in the air, the windier it is. This is why the strongest winds may blow in the warm tropics.*

. . . FASCINATING FACT . . .
The world's windiest place is George V in Antarctica, where 320 km/h winds are usual.

131

Tornadoes

- **Tornadoes,** or twisters, are long funnels of violently spiralling winds beneath thunderclouds.

- **Tornadoes** roar past in just a few minutes, but they can cause severe damage.

- **Wind speeds** inside tornadoes are difficult to measure, but they are believed to be over 400 km/h.

- **Tornadoes develop** beneath huge thunderclouds, called supercells, which develop along cold fronts.

- **England** has more tornadoes per square kilometre than any other country, but they are usually mild.

- **Tornado Alley** in Kansas, USA, has 1000 tornadoes a year. Some of them are immensely powerful.

▶ *Tornadoes are especially destructive in central USA but they can occur wherever there are thunderstorms.*

Supercell cloud

Funnel touches down in a whirling cloud of dust.

Cloud base

▶ *A tornado starts deep inside a thundercloud, where a column of strongly rising warm air is set spinning by high winds roaring through the cloud's top. As air is sucked into this column, or mesocyclone, it corkscrews down to the ground.*

- **A tornado** may be rated on the Fujita scale, from F0 (gale tornado) to F6 (inconceivable tornado).

- **An F5 tornado** (incredible tornado) can lift a house and carry a bus hundreds of metres.

- **In 1990** a Kansas tornado lifted an 88-car train from the track and then dropped it in piles four cars high.

...FASCINATING FACT...
In 1879, a Kansas tornado tore up an iron bridge and sucked dry the river beneath it.

Hurricanes

- **Hurricanes** are powerful, whirling tropical storms. They are also called willy-willies, cyclones or typhoons.

- **Hurricanes develop** in late summer as clusters of thunderstorms build up over warm seas (at least 27°C).

- **As hurricanes grow,** they tighten into a spiral with a calm ring of low pressure called the 'eye' at the centre.

- **Hurricanes** move westwards at about 20 km/h. They strike east coasts, bringing torrential rain and winds gusting up to 360 km/h.

- **Officially** a hurricane is a storm with winds exceeding 119 km/h.

- **Hurricanes** last, on average, 3–14 days. They die out as they move towards the Poles into cooler air.

- **Each hurricane** is given a name in alphabetical order each year, from a list issued by the World Meteorological Organization. The first storm of the year might be, for instance, Hurricane Andrew.

▶ *A satellite view of a hurricane approaching Florida, USA. Notice the yellow eye in the centre of the storm.*

▲ *The whirling winds of a hurricane can cause widespread destruction. The storm measures between 320 and 480 km in diameter.*

- **The most fatal cyclone ever** was the one that struck Bangladesh in 1970. It killed 266,000 with the flood from the storm surge – the rapid rise in sea level created as winds drive ocean waters ashore.

- **A hurricane** generates the same energy every second as a small hydrogen bomb.

- **Each year** 35 tropical storms reach hurricane status in the Atlantic Ocean, and 85 around the world.

Weather forecasting

- **Weather forecasting** relies partly on powerful computers, which analyse the Earth's atmosphere.

- **One kind of weather prediction** divides the air into parcels. These are stacked in columns above grid points spread throughout the world.

- **There are over one million** grid points. each grid point has a stack of at least 30 parcels above it.

▲ *Meteorologists use information from supercomputers to make weather forecasts for the next 24 hours and for up to a week ahead.*

136

▶ This weather map shows isobars – lines of equal air pressure – over North America. It has been compiled from millions of observations.

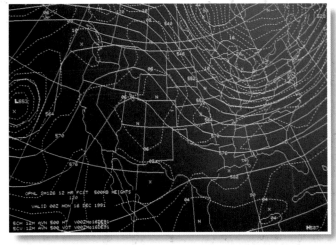

- **At regular intervals** each day, weather observatories take millions of simultaneous measurements of weather conditions.

- **Every three hours** 10,000 land-based weather stations record conditions on the ground. Every 12 hours balloons fitted with radiosondes go into the atmosphere to record conditions high up.

- **Satellites in the sky** give an overview of developing weather patterns.

- **Infrared satellite images** show temperatures on the Earth's surface.

- **Cloud motion winds** show the wind speed and wind direction from the way in which the clouds move.

- **Supercomputers** allow the weather to be predicted accurately three days in advance, and for up to 14 days in advance with some confidence.

- **Astrophysicist** Piers Corbyn has developed a forecasting system linked to variations in the Sun's activity.

Air pressure

- **Although air is light,** there is so much of it that air can exert huge pressure at ground level. Air pressure is the constant bombardment of billions of air molecules as they zoom about.

- **Air pushes** in all directions at ground level with a force of over 1 kg per sq cm – that is the equivalent of an elephant standing on a coffee table.

- **Air pressure varies** constantly from place to place and from time to time as the Sun's heat varies.

- **Air pressure** is measured with a device called a barometer in millibars.

- **Normal air pressure** at sea level is 1013 mb, but it can vary from between 800 mb and 1050 mb.

◄ *Barometers are used to detect changes in air pressure. The first barometer was invented by Evangelista Toricelli in 1644.*

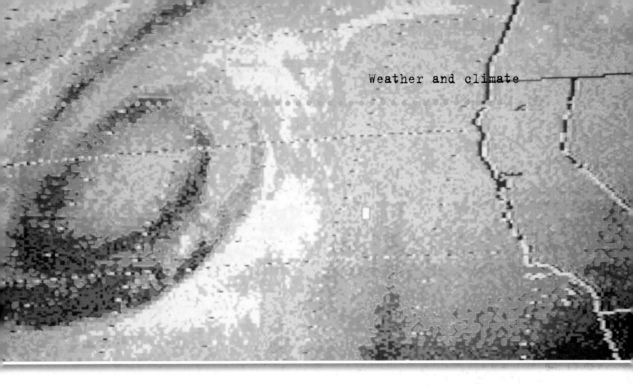

▲ *In this satellite picture, a spiral of clouds indicates that stormy weather in a depression is heading for California, USA.*

- **Air pressure** is shown on weather maps with lines called isobars, which join together places of equal pressure.

- **High-pressure zones** are called anticyclones; low-pressure zones are called cyclones, or depressions.

- **Barometers** help us to forecast weather because changes in air pressure are linked to changes in weather.

- **A fall in air pressure** warns that stormy weather is on its way, because depressions are linked to storms.

- **Steady high pressure** indicates clear weather, because sinking air in a high means that clouds cannot form.

Weather fronts

- **A weather front** is where a big mass of warm air meets a big mass of cold air.

- **At a warm front,** the mass of warm air is moving faster than the cold air. The warm air slowly rises over the cold air in a wedge. It slopes gently up to 1.5 km over 300 km.

- **At a cold front,** the mass of cold air is moving faster. It undercuts the warm air, forcing it to rise sharply and creating a steeply sloping front. The front climbs to 1.5 km over about 100 km.

- **In the mid-latitudes,** fronts are linked to vast spiralling weather systems called depressions, or lows. These are centred on a region of low pressure where warm, moist air rises. Winds spiral into the low – anticlockwise in the Northern Hemisphere, clockwise in the Southern.

- **Lows start** along the polar front, which stretches round the world. Here, cold air spreading out from the Poles meets warm, moist air moving up from the subtropics.

- **Lows develop** as a kink in the polar front. They then grow bigger as strong winds in the upper air drag them eastwards, bringing rain, snow and blustery winds. A wedge of warm air intrudes into the heart of the low, and the worst weather occurs along the edges of the wedge. One edge is a warm front, the other is a cold front.

- **The warm front arrives first,** heralded by feathery cirrus clouds of ice high in the sky. As the front moves over, the sky fills with slate-grey nimbostratus clouds that bring steady rain. As the warm front passes away, the weather becomes milder and skies may briefly clear.

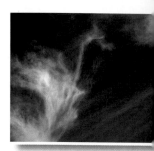

▲ *Feathery cirrus clouds high up in the sky are a clear warning that a warm front is on its way, bringing steady rain. When there is a warm front, a cold front is likely to follow, bringing heavy rain, strong winds and perhaps even a thunderstorm.*

- **After a few hours,** a build-up of thunderclouds and gusty winds warn that the cold front is on its way. When it arrives, the clouds unleash short, heavy showers, and sometimes thunderstorms or even tornadoes.

- **After the cold front passes,** the air grows colder and the sky clears, leaving just a few fluffy cumulus clouds.

- **Meteorologists** think that depressions are linked to strong winds, called jet streams, which circle the Earth high above the polar front. The depression may begin with Rossby waves, which are giant kinks in the jet stream up to 2000 km long.

▼ *This illustration shows two short sections through the cold and warm weather fronts that are linked to depressions in the mid-latitudes.*

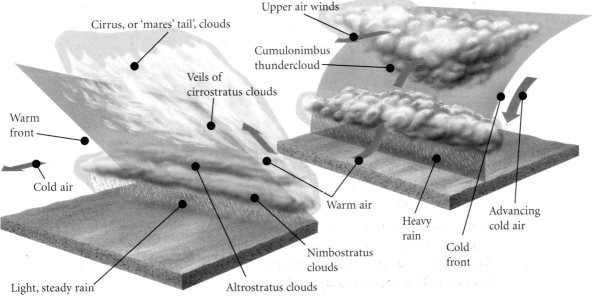

Cirrus, or 'mares' tail', clouds

Upper air winds

Cumulonimbus thundercloud

Veils of cirrostratus clouds

Warm front

Cold air

Warm air

Heavy rain

Advancing cold air

Cold front

Light, steady rain

Nimbostratus clouds

Altrostratus clouds

Air pollution

▲ *Factories pour out a range of fumes that pollute the air.*

- **Air pollution** comes mainly from car, bus and truck exhausts, waste burners, factories, power stations and the burning of oil, coal and gas in homes.

- **Air pollution** can also come from farmers' crop sprays, farm animals, mining and volcanic eruptions.

- **Some pollutants,** such as soot and ash, are solid, but many more pollutants are gases.

- **Air pollution** can spread huge distances. Pesticides, for instance, have been discovered in Antarctica where they have never been used.

- **Most fuels** are chemicals called hydrocarbons. Any hydrocarbons that are left unburned can react in sunlight to form toxic ozone.

► *The increased use of cars has made air pollution a serious problem, particularly in the world's largest cities.*

- **When exhaust gases** react in strong sunlight to form ozone, they may create a photochemical smog.

> **...FASCINATING FACT...**
> Factories in the Chinese city of Benxi make so much smoke the city is invisible to satellites.

- **Air pollution** is probably a major cause of global warming (see global warming).

- **Air pollution** may destroy the ozone layer inside the Earth's atmosphere (see the ozone hole).

- **Breathing the air** in Mexico City is thought to be as harmful as smoking 40 cigarettes a day.

143

Acid rain

▲ *Cuts in emissions are essential to reduce acid rain, but installing 'scrubbers' that soak up sulphur and nitrous oxide are expensive.*

- **All rain** is slightly acidic, but air pollution can turn rain into harmful acid rain.

- **Acid rain** forms when sunlight makes sulphur dioxide and nitrogen oxide combine with oxygen and moisture in the air.

- **Sulphur dioxide and nitrogen oxides** come from burning fossil fuels such as coal, oil and natural gas.

- **Acidity** is measured in terms of pH. The lower the pH, the more acid the rain is. Normal rain has a pH of 6.5. Acid rain has a pH of 5.7 or less.

- **A pH** of 2–3 has been recorded in many places in the eastern USA and central Europe.

- **Acid fog** is ten times more acid than acid rain.

...FASCINATING FACT...
Sulphur emissions from ships may double by 2010, counteracting cuts in power station emissions.

- **Acid rain** washes aluminium from soil into lakes and streams, and so poisons fish. Limestone helps to neutralize the acid, but granite areas are vulnerable. Spring meltwaters are especially acid and damaging.

- **Acid rain** damages plants by removing nutrients from leaves and blocking the plants' uptake of nitrogen.

- **Acid rain has damaged** 20% of European trees; in Germany 60% of trees have been damaged.

▲ *Acid rain pollutes streams, rivers and lakes killing fish and other aquatic life.*

145

The ozone hole

▲ *Meteorologists predict the world temperature will rise between 2 and 4°C by 2030 unless we cut the amount of greenhouse gases we produce.*

- **Life on Earth** depends on the layer of ozone gas in the air (see atmosphere), which shields the Earth from the Sun's ultraviolet (UV) rays. Ozone molecules are made from three atoms of oxygen, not two like oxygen.

- **In 1982** scientists in Antarctica noticed a 50% loss of ozone over the Antarctic every spring. This finding was confirmed in 1985 by the Nimbus-7 satellite.

- **The ozone hole** is a patch where the ozone layer becomes very thin.

- **The ozone hole** appears over Antarctica every spring.

- **The ozone hole** is monitored all the time by the TOMS (Total Ozone Mapping Spectrometer) satellite.

- **The loss of ozone** is caused by manufactured gases, notably chlorofluorocarbons (CFCs), which drift up through the air and combine with the ozone.

- **CFCs** are used in many things, from refrigerators and acrosol sprays to forming the foam for fast-food cartons.

- **CFCs** were banned in 1996, but it may be at least 100 years before the ban takes effect. The hole is still growing.

- **UV rays** from the Sun come in three kinds: UVA, UVB and UVC. Both oxygen and ozone soak up UVA and UVC rays, but only ozone absorbs UVB. For every 1% loss of ozone, 1% more UVB rays reach the Earth's surface.

▼*The loss of ozone was first spotted by scientists in the Antarctic.*

Global warming

▲ *Could global warming make the Mediterranean look like this?*

- **Global warming** is the increase in average temperatures around the world. This increase has been between 0.3°C and 0.8°C over the 20th century.

- **Most scientists** now think that global warming is caused by human activities, which have resulted in an increase in the Earth's natural greenhouse effect.

- **The greenhouse effect** is the way that certain gases in the air – notably carbon dioxide – trap some of the Sun's warmth, like the panes of glass in the walls and roof of a greenhouse.

▶ *The greenhouse effect occurs when carbon dioxide is released into the atmosphere by burning coal and oil (fossil fuels).*

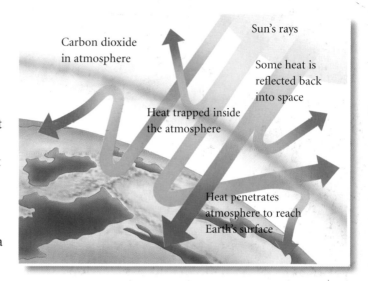

Carbon dioxide in atmosphere

Sun's rays

Some heat is reflected back into space

Heat trapped inside the atmosphere

Heat penetrates atmosphere to reach Earth's surface

- **The greenhouse effect** keeps the Earth pleasantly warm – but if it increases, the Earth may become very hot.

- **Many experts** expect a 4°C rise in average temperatures over the next 100 years.

- **Humans** boost the greenhouse effect by burning fossil fuels, such as coal, oil and natural gas that produce carbon dioxide.

- **Emission of the greenhouse gas** methane from the world's cattle has added to the increase in global warming.

- **Global warming** is bringing stormier weather by trapping more energy inside the atmosphere.

- **Global warming** may melt much of the polar ice caps, flooding low-lying countries such as Bangladesh.

... **FASCINATING FACT** ...
Recent observations show global warming could be much worse than we thought.

149

Continental drift

- **Continental drift** is the slow movement of the continents around the world.

- **About 220 million years ago** all the continents were joined together in one supercontinent, which geologists call Pangaea.

- **Pangaea** began to break up about 200 million years ago. The fragments slowly drifted apart to form the continents we know today.

- **South America** used to be joined to Africa and North America to Europe.

- **The first hint** that the continents were once joined was the discovery by German explorer Alexander von Humboldt (1769–1859) that rocks in Brazil (South America) and the Congo (Africa) are very similar.

- **When German meteorologist** Alfred Wegener (1880–1930) suggested the idea of continental drift in 1923, many scientists laughed. The chairman of the American Philosophical Society described the idea as 'Utter damned rot!'

- **Strong evidence** of continental drift has come from similar ancient fossils found in separate continents, such as the Glossopteris fern found in both Australia and India; the Diadectid insect found in Europe and North America; and Lystrosaurus, a tropical reptile from 200 million years ago, found in Africa, India, China and Antarctica.

- **Satellites** provide incredibly accurate ways of measuring, they can actually measure the slow movement of the continents. The main method is satellite laser ranging (SLR), which involves bouncing a laser beam off a satellite from ground stations on each continent. Other methods include using the Global Positioning System and Very Long Baseline Interferometry.

- **Rates of continental drift** vary. India drifted north into Asia very quickly. South America is moving 20 cm farther from Africa every year. On average, continents move at about the same rate as a fingernail grows.

...FASCINATING FACT...
New York is moving about 2.5 cm farther
away from London every year.

1. About 220 million years ago, all
the continents were joined in the
supercontinent of Pangaea. It was
surrounded by a single giant ocean
called Panthalassa, meaning 'all seas'.

▼ It is hard to believe that the continents move, but they do. Over tens
of millions of years they move huge distances. The drifting of the
continents has changed the map of the world very, very slowly over the
past 200 million years, and will continue to do so in the future.

3. About 110 million years ago North and
South America finally began to link up. Later,
Australia and Antarctica separated. India broke
off from Africa and drifted rapidly north into
Asia. Europe and North America began to
move apart about 60 million years ago, at
about the same time that the
dinosaurs died out.

2. By 200 million years
ago Pangaea had split into
two huge landmasses called
Laurasia and Gondwanaland,
separated by the Tethys Sea.
About 135 million years ago these
landmasses also began to divide.

4. The continents have not stopped moving.
North America is still moving farther away
from Europe – and closer to Asia.

151

Europe

▲ *Tourism plays an important part in the economy of the countries around the Mediterranean.*

- **Europe** is the smallest continent, with an area of just 10,400,000 sq km. For its size Europe has an immensely long coastline.

- **In the north** are the ancient glaciated mountains of Scandinavia and Scotland, which were once much, much higher.

- **Across the centre** are the lowlands of the North European Plain, stretching from the Urals in Russia to France in the west.

- **Much of southern Europe** has been piled up into young mountain ranges, as Africa drifts north.

- **The highest point** in Europe is Mt Elbrus in the Russian Caucasus, 5642 m high.

- **Northwest Europe** was once joined to Canada. The ancient Caledonian mountains of eastern Canada, Greenland, Scandinavia and Scotland were formed together as a single mountain chain 360–540 million years ago.

- **Mediterranean Europe** has a Mediterranean climate with warm summers and mild winters.

- **NW Europe** is often wet and windy. It has very mild winters because it is bathed by the warm North Atlantic Drift (see ocean currents).

▲ *Europe is a small continent but its peninsulas and inlets give it a long coast.*

- **The Russian islands** of Novaya Zimlya are far into the Arctic Circle and are icebound in winter.

- **The largest lake** is Ladoga in Russia, 18,389 sq km.

153

Australasia

▲ *The Great Barrier Reef is home to over 1500 species of fish.*

- **Australasia** is a vast region that includes islands spread over much of the Pacific Ocean. The land area is 8,508,238 sq km. However the total sea area is much, much bigger.

- **Australia** is the only country in the world which is also a continent in its own right.

- **The largest island** is New Guinea which has a total area of 787,878 sq km.

- **Fraser Island,** off Queensland, Australia, is the world's largest sand island with a sand dune 120 km long.

- **Australasia** is mostly tropical, with temperatures averaging 30°C in the north of Australia, and slightly lower on the islands where the ocean keeps the land cool.

- **New Zealand** is only a few thousand kilometres from the Antarctic Circle at its southern tip. As a result of occupying this position New Zealand has only mild summers and cold winters.

- **Australasia's highest peak** is Mt Wilhelm on Papua New Guinea, 4300 m high.

- **The Great Barrier Reef** is the world's largest living thing, 2027 km long. It is the only structure built by animals that is visible from space.

- **Australia** was the first continent to break off from Pangaea (see continental drift) about 200 million years ago, and so has developed its own unique wildlife.

- **Australia sits** on the Indian – Australian plate, which is moving very slowly north away from Antarctica. New Zealand sits astride the boundary (see converging plates) with the Pacific plate.

▲ *Apart from the landmass of Australia, much of Australasia is open water.*

155

Asia

- **Asia is the world's largest continent,** stretching from Europe in the west to Japan in the east. It has a total area of 44,680,718 sq km.

- **Asia has huge climate extremes,** from a cold polar climate in the north to a hot tropical one in the south.

- **Verkhoyansk** in Siberia has had temperatures as high as 37°C and as low as −68°C.

- **The Himalayas** are the highest mountains in the world, with 14 peaks over 8000 m high. To the north are vast empty deserts, broad grasslands and huge coniferous forests. To the south are fertile plains and valleys and steamy tropical jungles.

- **Northern Asia** sits on one giant tectonic plate.

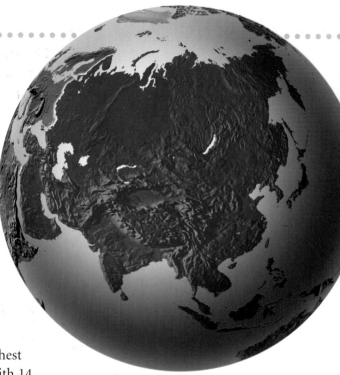

▲ *Asia is a vast continent of wide plains and dark forests in the north, separated from the tropical south by the Himalayas.*

...**FASCINATING FACT**...
Lake Baikal is the world's deepest lake – 1743m – and it holds 20% of the world's fresh water.

- **India** is on a separate plate that crashed into the north Asia plate 50 million years ago. It is piling up the Himalayas as it ploughs on northwards.

- **Asia's longest river** is China's Yangtze, 5520 km long.

- **Asia's** highest mountain is the world's highest – Mt Everest, or Sagarmatha, in Nepal at 8848 m.

- **The Caspian Sea** between Azerbaijan and Kazakhstan is the world's largest lake, covering 378,400 sq km.

▲ *Lake Baikal in Siberia, Russia, is about 25 million years old. It contains about one-fifth of all the world's fresh water. The water is carried there by 336 rivers that flow into it. Lake Baikal has the world's only freshwater seals, and among its many unique animals is a fish that bears live young.*

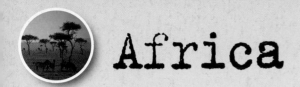

Africa

- **Africa is the world's second largest** continent. It stretches from the Mediterranean in the north to the Cape of Good Hope in the south. It has a total area of 30,131,536 sq km.

- **Africa is the world's warmest** continent, lying almost entirely within the tropics or subtropics.

- **Temperatures in the Sahara Desert** are the highest on Earth, often soaring over 50°C.

- **The Sahara** in the north of Africa, and the Kalahari in the south, are the world's largest deserts. Most of the continent in between is savannah (grassland) and bush. In the west and centre are lush rainforests.

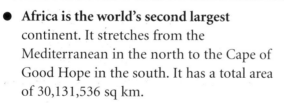

▲ Africa is a vast, warm, fairly flat continent covered in savannah, desert and tropical forest.

▲ *In the savannah (grassland) trees and bushes are scarce and new grass only grows when the rainy season comes.*

> **... FASCINATING FACT ...**
> The river Nile is the world's longest river, measuring 6738 km long.

- **Much of Africa** consists of vast plains and plateaux, broken in places by mountains such as the Atlas range in the northwest and the Ruwenzori in the centre.

- **The Great Rift Valley** runs 7200 km from the Red Sea. It is a huge gash in the Earth's surface opened up by the pulling apart of two giant tectonic plates.

- **Africa's largest lake** is Victoria, 69,484 sq km.

- **Africa's highest mountain** is Kilimanjaro, 5895 m high.

- **The world's** biggest sand dune is 430 m high – Erg Tifernine in Algeria.

North America

▶ *North America broke away from Europe about 100 million years ago. It is still moving 2.5 cm farther every year.*

- **North America** is the world's third largest continent. It has an area of 24,230,000 sq km.

- **North America** is a triangle, with its long side bounded by the icy Arctic Ocean and its short side by the tropical Caribbean Sea.

- **The north** of North America lies inside the Arctic Circle and is icebound for much of the year. Death Valley, in the southwestern desert in California and Nevada, is one of the hottest places on the Earth.

- **Mountain ranges** run down each side of North America – the ancient, worn-down Appalachians in the east and the younger, higher Rockies in the west.

- **In between** the mountains lie vast interior plains. These plains are based on very old rocks, the oldest of which are in the Canadian Shield in the north.

● **North America** is the oldest continent on the Earth. It has rocks that are almost 4000 million years old.

● **The Grand Canyon** is one of the world's most spectacular gorges. It is 440 km long, and 1800 m deep in places.

● **The longest river** in North America is the Mississippi–Missouri, at 6019 km long.

● **The highest mountain** is Mt McKinley in Alaska, 6,194 m high.

● **The Great Lakes** contain one fifth of the world's fresh water.

▼ *The Grand Canyon covers almost 500,000 hectares. It is one of North America's most popular tourist attractions.*

South America

▲ *The Amazon rainforest covers an area of about 6 million sq km.*

- **South America** is the world's fourth largest continent. It has a total area of 17,814,000 sq km.

- **The Andes Mountains,** which run over 4500 km down the west side, are the world's longest mountain range.

- **The heart of South America** is the vast Amazon rainforest around the Amazon River and its tributaries.

- **The southeast** is dominated by the huge grasslands of the Gran Chaco, the Pampas and Patagonia.

- **No other continent** reaches so far south. South America extends to within 1000 km of the Antarctic Circle.

- **Three-quarters of South America** is in the tropics. In the high Andes are large zones of cool, temperate climate.

- **Quito, in Ecuador** is called the 'Land of Eternal Spring' because its temperature never drops below 8°C at night, and never climbs above 22°C during the day.

- **The highest volcanic peak** in South America is Aconcagua, 6960 m high.

- **Eastern South America** was joined to western Africa until the Atlantic began to open up 90 million years ago.

- **The Andes** have been built up over the past 60 million years by the collision of the South American plate with both the Nazca plate under the Pacific Ocean and the Caribbean plate. The subduction of the Nazca plate has created the world's highest active volcanoes in the Andes.

▲ *South America's triangular shape gives it the shortest coastline, for its size, of any of the continents.*

Antarctica

▲ *Antarctica does not belong to any one nation. Under the Antarctic Treaty of 1959, 12 countries agreed to use it only for scientific research.*

- **Antarctica** is the ice-covered continent at the South Pole. It covers an area of 14 million square km and is larger than Australia.

- **It is the coldest place** on Earth. Even in summer, temperatures rarely climb over −25°C. On July 21, 1983, the air at the Vostok science station plunged to −89.2°C.

- **Antarctica** is one of the driest places on Earth, with barely any rain or snow. It is also very windy.

▶ *This map shows the current international claims on Antarctica made by seven countries.*

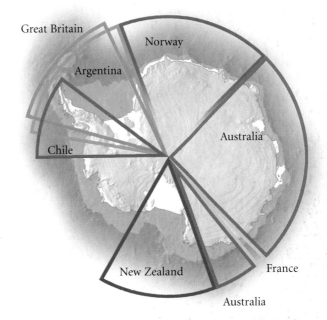

- **Until about 80 million years ago** Antarctica was joined to Australia.

- **Glaciers began to form** in Antarctica 38 million years ago, and grew rapidly from 13 million years ago. For the past five million years 98% of the continent has been covered in ice.

- **The Antarctic ice cap** contains 70% of the world's fresh water.

- **The ice cap** is thickest – up to 4800 m deep – in deep sea basins dipping far below the surface. Here it is thick enough to bury the Alps.

- **Antarctica** is mountainous. Its highest point is the Vinson Massif, 5140 m high, but there are many peaks over 4000 m in the Transarctic Range.

- **The magnetic South Pole** – the pole to which a compass needle points – moves 8 km a year.

- **Fossils of tropical plants** and reptiles show that Antarctica was at one time in the tropics.

165

Mountain ranges

▲ *Mountain ranges are thrown up by the crumpling of rock strata (layers) as the tectonic plates of the Earth's surface crunch together.*

- **Great mountain ranges** such as the Andes in South America usually lie along the edges of continents.

- **Most mountain ranges** are made by the folding of rock layers (see folds) as tectonic plates move slowly together.

- **High ranges** are geologically young because they are soon worn down. The Himalayas are 25 million years old.

- **Many ranges** are still growing. The Himalayas grow a few centimetres each year as the Indian plate pushes into Asia.

- **Mountain-building** is very slow because rocks flow like thick treacle. Rock is pushed up like the bow wave in front of a boat as one tectonic plate pushes into another.

- **Satellite techniques** show that the central peaks of the Andes and Himalayas are rising. The outer peaks are sinking as the rock flows slowly away from the 'bow wave'.

- **Mountain-building** is very active during orogenic (mountain-forming) phases that last millions of years.

- **Different orogenic phases** occur in different places, for example the Caledonian, Hercynian and Alpine in Europe and the Huronian, Nevadian and Pasadenian in North America. The Caledonian was about 550 million years ago.

- **Mountain-building** makes the Earth's crust especially thick under mountains, giving them very deep 'roots'.

- **As mountains** are worn down, their weight reduces and the 'roots' float upwards. This is called isostasy.

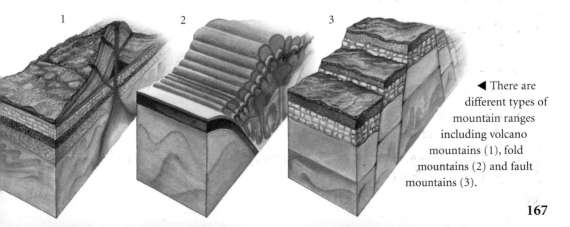

◀ There are different types of mountain ranges including volcano mountains (1), fold mountains (2) and fault mountains (3).

High mountains

- **A few high mountains** are lone volcanoes, such as Africa's Kilimanjaro, which are built by many eruptions.

- **Some volcanic mountains** are in chains in volcanic arcs (see volcano zones), such as Japan's Fujiyama.

- **Most high mountains** are part of great mountain ranges stretching over hundreds of kilometres.

- **Some mountain ranges** are huge slabs of rock called fault blocks (see faults). They were forced up by quakes.

- **The biggest mountain ranges,** such as the Himalayas and the Andes, are fold mountain ranges.

▼ *High peaks are jagged because massive folding fractures the rock and makes it very vulnerable to the sharp frosts high up.*

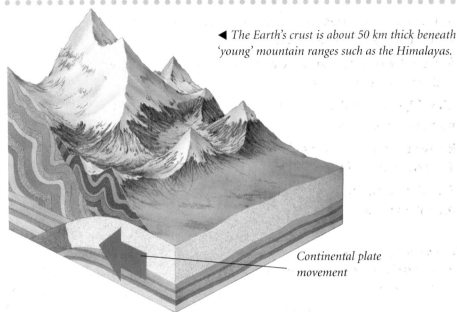

◀ *The Earth's crust is about 50 km thick beneath 'young' mountain ranges such as the Himalayas.*

Continental plate movement

- **The height of mountains** used to be measured from the ground, using levels and sighting devices to measure angles. Now mountains are measured more accurately using satellite techniques.

- **Satellite measurements** in 1999 raised the height of the world's highest peak, Mt Everest in Nepal in the Himalayas, from 8848 m to 8850 m.

- **All 14 of the world's peaks** over 8000 m are in the Himalayas – in Nepal, China and Kashmir.

- **Temperatures drop 0.6°C** for every 100 m you climb, so mountain peaks are very cold and often covered in snow.

- **The air** is thinner on mountains, so the air pressure is lower. Climbers may need oxygen masks to breathe.

169

Great rivers

- **Measurements** of river lengths vary according to where the river is said to begin. So some people say that Africa's Nile is the world's longest river; others say that South America's Amazon is longer.

- **The source** of the Amazon was only discovered in 1971, in snowbound lakes high in the Andes. It is named Laguna McIntyre after the American who found it.

▲ *All great rivers develop the same horseshoe-shaped meanders in their lower reaches (see river channels).*

- **If the full length** of the Amazon is counted, it is 6750 km long compared with the Nile at 6670 km.

- **The Amazon basin** covers more than 7 million sq km.

- **China's Yangtse** is the third longest river, at 6300 km.

- **The world's longest tributary** is the Madeira flowing into the Amazon. At 3380 km long it is the 18th longest river in the world.

> ....FASCINATING FACT....
> The Amazon in flood could fill the world's biggest sports stadium with water in 13 seconds.

▲ *The river Seine in Paris runs under more than 30 bridges.*

- **The world's longest estuary** is that of the Ob in Russia, which is up to 80 km wide and 885 km long.

- **The Ob** is the biggest river to freeze solid in winter.

- **The shortest official river** is the North Fork Roe River in Montana, USA, which is just 17.7 m long.

171

Great lakes

- **Most of the world's great lakes** lie in regions that were once glaciated. The glaciers carved out deep hollows in the rock in which water collected. The Great Lakes of the USA and Canada are partly glacial in origin.

- **In Minnesota, USA** 11,000 lakes were formed by glaciers.

- **The world's deepest lakes** are often formed by faults in the Earth's crust, such as Lake Baikal in Siberia (see Asia) and Lake Tanganyika in East Africa.

▲ *Many of the world's great lakes were formed by glaciation, and will eventually disappear.*

- **Most lakes** last only a few thousand years before they are filled in by silt or drained by changes in the landscape.

- **The world's oldest great lake** is Lake Baikal in Siberia, which is over 2 million years old.

- **The Great Lakes** include three of the world's five largest lakes: Superior, Huron and Michigan.

- **The world's largest lake** is the Caspian Sea (see Asia), which is a huge saltwater lake below sea level. It covers 371,000 sq km.

- **The world's highest great lake** is Lake Titicaca in South America, which is 3812 m above sea level.

- **The world's lowest great lake** is the Dead Sea between Israel and Jordan. It is 399 m below sea level and getting lower all the time.

- **The largest underground lake** in the world is Drauchen-hauchloch, which is inside a cave in Namibia.

▶ *The Great Lakes are the world's largest group of freshwater lakes. They contain 18 % of the world's fresh surface water.*

Biomes

◀ *Extreme conditions, such as flooding in a swamp, can create different kinds of communities within the same biome.*

- **A biome** is a community of plants and animals adapted to similar conditions in certain parts of the world.

- **Biomes** are also known as 'major life zones' or 'biogeographical regions'.

- **The soil** and animal life of a region is closely linked to its vegetation. Biomes are usually named after the dominant vegetation, e.g. grassland or coniferous forest.

- **Vegetation** is closely linked to climate, so biomes correspond to climate zones.

- **Major biome types** include: tundra, boreal (cold) coniferous forests, temperate deciduous forests, temperate grasslands, savannahs (tropical grasslands), tropical rainforests and deserts.

- **Most types of biome** are found across several different continents.

- **Species within a biome type** vary from continent to continent, but they share the same kind of vegetation.

▲ *Savannah, grassy plains with scattered trees, covers over two-fifths of the land in Africa.*

- **Many plants and animals** have features that make them especially suited to a particular biome.

- **Polar bears** are adapted to life in the Arctic; cacti are well equipped to survive in the desert.

- **Biomes also exist in the sea,** for example coral reefs.

175

Ecosystems

- **An ecosystem** is a community of living things interacting with each other and their surroundings.

- **An ecosystem** can be anything from a piece of rotting wood to a huge swamp. In every ecosystem each organism depends on the others.

- **When vegetation** colonizes an area, the first plants to grow there are small and simple, such as mosses and lichens. Grass and sedges appear next.

- **The simple plants** stabilize the soil so that bigger and more complex plants can move in. This is called vegetation succession.

- **Rainforest ecosystems** cover only 8% of the world's land, yet they include 40% of all the world's plant and animal species.

- **Farming has a huge effect** on natural ecosystems, reducing the number of species dramatically.

- **Green plants** are autotrophs, or producers, which means they make their own food (from sunlight).

▶ *Rainforests are the world's richest and most threatened regions.*

- **Animals** are heterotrophs, or consumers, which means they get their food from other living things.
- **Primary consumers** are herbivores that eat plants.
- **Secondary consumers** are carnivores that eat herbivores or each other.

◀ *How vegetation may develop in a deciduous woodland. This process is called vegetation succession.*

Seas

- **Seas** are small oceans, completely enclosed or partly enclosed by land.

- **Seas** are shallower than oceans and have do not have any major currents flowing through them.

- **In the Mediterranean** and other seas, tides can set up a seiche – a standing wave that sloshes back and forth like a ripple running up and down a bath.

- **If the natural** wave cycle of a seiche is different from the ocean tides, the tides are cancelled out.

- **If the natural** wave cycle of a seiche is similar to the ocean tides, the tides are magnified.

- **Scientists thought that** the Mediterranean was a dry desert 6 million years ago. They believed it was 3000 m lower than it is today, and covered in salts.

▲ *The warm waters of the Mediterranean attract tourists to the coast of Spain.*

- **Recent evidence** from microfossils suggests that the Mediterranean was never completely dry.

- **Warm seas such as the Mediterranean** lose much more water by evaporation than they gain from rivers. So a current of water flows in steadily from the ocean.

- **Warm seas** lose so much water by evaporation that they are usually much saltier than the open ocean.

▼ *Waves in enclosed seas tend to be much smaller than those in the open ocean, because there is less space for them to develop.*

...FASCINATING FACT...
The Dead Sea is the lowest sea on Earth, 400 m below sea level.

The Pacific Ocean

- **The Pacific** is the world's largest ocean. It is twice as large as the Atlantic and covers over one third of the world, with an area of 181 million sq km.

- **It is over 24,000 km** across from Panama to the Malay Peninsula – more than halfway round the world.

- **The word 'pacific'** means calm. The ocean got its name from the 16th-century Portuguese explorer Magellan who was lucky enough to find gentle winds.

- **The Pacific is dotted** with thousands of islands. Some are the peaks of undersea volcanoes. Others are coral reefs sitting on top of the peaks.

▲ *There are thousands of of low lying islands in the Pacific .Most are only about a metre above sea level.*

◄ *The coastal waters of California are rich in petroleum – the most important mineral resource of the Pacific.*

- **The Pacific** has some of the greatest tides in the world (over 9 m off Korea). Its smallest tide (just 0.3 m) is on Midway Island in the middle of the Pacific.

- **On average,** the Pacific Ocean is 4200 m deep.

- **Around the rim** there are deep ocean trenches including the world's deepest, the Mariana Trench.

- **A huge** undersea mountain range called the East Pacific Rise stretches from Antarctica up to Mexico.

- **The floor of the Pacific** is spreading along the East Pacific Rise at the rate of 12–16 cm per year.

- **The Pacific** has more seamounts (undersea mountains) than any other ocean.

181

The Atlantic Ocean

▲ *The damp, cool climate of the northern Atlantic frequently turns its waters steely grey.*

- **The Atlantic Ocean** is the world's second largest ocean, with an area of 82 million sq km. It covers about one-fifth of the world's surface.

- **At its widest point,** between Spain and Mexico, the Atlantic is 9600 km across.

- **The Atlantic** was named by the ancient Romans after the Atlas Mountains of North Africa.

- **There are very few islands** in the main part of the Atlantic Ocean. Most lie close to the continents.

- **On average,** the Atlantic is about 3660 m deep.

- **The deepest point** in the Atlantic is the Puerto Rico Trench off Puerto Rico, which is 8648 m deep.

- **The Mid-Atlantic Ridge** is a great undersea ridge which splits the sea-bed in half. Along this ridge, the Atlantic is growing wider by 2–4 cm every year.

- **Islands** in the mid-Atlantic are volcanoes that lie along the Mid-Atlantic Ridge, such as the Azores and Ascension Island.

- **The Sargasso Sea** is a huge area of water in the western Atlantic. It is famous for its floating seaweed.

- **The Atlantic** is a youngish ocean, about 150 million years old.

▲ *The Atlantic Ocean provides around a quarter of the world's catch of fish.*

The Indian Ocean

▼ *Many of the Indian Ocean's islands have coral beaches.*

- **The Indian Ocean** is the third largest ocean. It is about half the size of the Pacific Ocean and covers one fifth of the world's ocean area. It has a total area of 73,426,000 sq km.

- **The average depth** of the Indian Ocean is 3890 m.

- **The deepest point** is the Java Trench off Java, in Indonesia, which is 7450 m deep. It marks the line where the Australian plate is being subducted (see converging plates) under the Eurasian plate.

- **The Indian Ocean** is 10,000 km across at its widest point, between Africa and Australia.

- **Scientists believe** that the Indian Ocean began to form about 200 million years ago when Australia broke away from Africa, followed by India.

- **The Indian Ocean** is getting 20 cm wider every year.

- **The Indian Ocean** is scattered with thousands of tropical islands such as the Seychelles and Maldives.

- **The Maldives** are so low lying that they may be swamped if global warming melts the polar ice.

- **Unlike in other oceans,** currents in the Indian Ocean change course twice a year. They are blown by monsoon winds towards Africa in winter, and then in the other direction towards India in summer.

- **The Persian Gulf** is the warmest sea in the world; the Red Sea is the saltiest.

▶ *In the warm waters of the Indian Ocean coral reefs flourish.*

The Arctic Ocean

▲ *Icebreakers are able to smash their way through sea ice using the strength of their reinforced bows.*

- **Most of the Arctic Ocean** is permanently covered with a vast floating raft of sea ice.

- **Temperatures** are low all year round, averaging – 30°C in winter and sometimes dropping to – 70°C.

- **During the long winters,** which last more than four months, the Sun never rises above the horizon.

- **The Arctic** gets its name from arctos, the Greek word for 'bear', because the Great Bear constellation is above the North Pole.

- **There are three kinds of sea ice** in the Arctic: polar ice, pack ice and fast ice.

- **Polar ice** is the raft of ice that never melts through.

- **Polar ice** may be as thin as 2 m in places in summer, but in winter it is up to 50 m thick.

- **Pack ice** forms around the edge of the polar ice and only freezes completely in winter.

- **The ocean swell** breaks and crushes the pack ice into chunky ice blocks and fantastic ice sculptures.

- **Fast ice** forms in winter between pack ice and the land around the Arctic Ocean. It gets its name because it is held fast to the shore. It cannot move up and down with the ocean as the pack ice does.

▲ *The seal is one of the few creatures that can survive the bitter cold of the Arctic winter.*

The Southern Ocean

- **The Southern Ocean** is the world's fourth largest ocean. It stretches all the way round Antarctica, and has an area of 35,000,000 sq km.

- **It is the only ocean** that stretches all around the world.

- **In winter** over half the Southern Ocean is covered with ice and icebergs that break off the Antarctic ice sheet.

- **The East Wind Drift** is a current that flows anticlockwise around Antarctica close to the coast.

- **Further out** from the coast of Antarctica, the Antarctic circumpolar current flows in the opposite direction – clockwise from west to east.

- **The circumpolar current** carries more water than any other current in the world.

▲ *Many penguins such as the Emperor, the world's largest penguin, live on the ice floes of the Southern Ocean.*

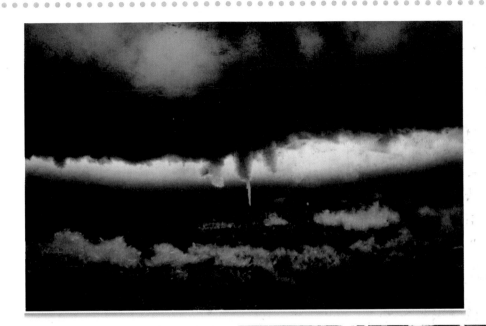

▲ *Beneath the surface of the Antarctic ice, the sea temperature reaches just -2°C. The freezing water is also a rich source of krill – tiny shrimp-like creatures.*

...FASCINATING FACT...
The circumpolar current could fill the Great Lakes in North America in just 48 hours.

- **The 'Roaring Forties'** is the band between 40° and 50° South latitude. Within this band strong westerly winds blow unobstructed around the world.

- **The waves in the 'Roaring Forties'** are the biggest in the world, sometimes higher than a ten-storey building.

- **Sea ice** forms in round pieces called pancake ice.

189

Beaches

- **Beaches** are sloping bands of sand, shingle or pebbles along the edge of a sea or lake.

- **Some beaches** are made entirely of broken coral or shells.

- **On a steep beach,** the backwash after each wave is strong. It washes material down the beach and so makes the beach gentler sloping.

- **On a gently sloping beach,** each wave runs in powerfully and falls back gently. Material gets washed up the beach, making it steeper.

> ...FASCINATING FACT...
> The world's largest pleasure beach is Virginia Beach, Virginia, USA, over 45 km long.

▶ *Waves crashing against the shore can weaken cliffs and cause some to fall into the sea.*

▲ *The little bays in this beach have been scooped out as waves strike the beach at an angle.*

- **The slope of a beach** matches the waves, so the slope is often gentler in winter when the waves are stronger.

- **A storm beach** is a ridge of gravel and pebbles flung high above the normal high-tide mark during a storm.

- **At the top of each beach** a ridge, or berm, is often left at the high-tide mark.

- **Beach cusps** are tiny bays in the sand that are scooped out along the beach when waves strike it at an angle.

- **Many scientists** believe that beaches are only a temporary phenomenon caused by the changes in sea levels after the last Ice Age.

191

Coasts

- **Coastlines** are changing all the time as new waves roll in and out and tides rise and fall every six hours or so. Over longer periods coastlines are reshaped by the action of waves and the corrosion of salty water.

- **On exposed coasts** where waves strike the high rocks, they undercut the slope to create steep cliffs and headlands. Often waves can penetrate into the cliff to open up sea caves or blast through arches. When a sea arch collapses, it leaves behind tall pillars called stacks which may be worn away to stumps.

- **Waves work** on rocks in two ways. First, the rocks are pounded with a huge weight of water filled with stones. Second, the waves force air into cracks in the rocks with such force that the rocks split apart.

- **The erosive power** of waves is focused in a narrow band at wave height. So as waves wear away sea cliffs, they leave the rock below wave height untouched. As cliffs retreat, the waves slice away a broad shelf of rock called a wave-cut platform. Water left behind in dips when the tide falls forms rockpools.

- **On more sheltered coasts,** the sea may pile up sand into beaches (see beaches). The sand has been washed down by rivers or worn away from cliffs.

- **When waves hit** a beach at an angle, they fall straight back down the beach at a right angle. Any sand and shingle that the waves carry fall back slightly farther along the beach. In this way sand and shingle are moved along the beach in a zig-zag fashion. This is called longshore drift.

- **On beaches** prone to longshore drift, low fences called groynes are often built to stop the sand being washed away along the beach.

- **Longshore drift** can wash sand out across bays and estuaries to create sand bars called spits.

- **Bays** are broad indents in the coast with a headland on each side. Waves reach the headlands first, focusing their energy here. Material is worn away from the headlands and washed into the bay, forming a bay-head beach.

- **A cove is a small bay.** A bight is a huge bay, such as the Great Australian Bight. A gulf is a long narrow bight. The world's biggest bay is Hudson Bay, Canada, which has a shoreline 12,268 km long. The Bay of Bengal in India is larger in area.

▼ *The main features of a coastline.*

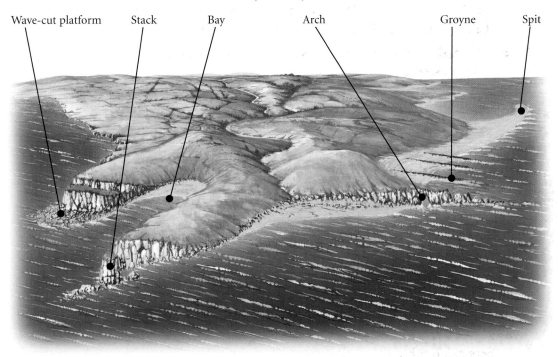

Wave-cut platform   Stack   Bay   Arch   Groyne   Spit

Waves

- **Waves in the sea** are formed when wind blows across the sea and whips the surface into ripples.

- **Water particles** are dragged a short way by the friction between air and water, which is known as wind stress.

- **If the wind continues to blow** long and strong enough in the same direction, moving particles may build up into a ridge of water. At first this is a ripple, then a wave.

- **Waves seem to move** but the water in them stays in the same place, rolling around like rollers on a conveyor belt.

- **The size of a wave** depends on the strength of the wind and how far it blows over the water (the fetch).

▲ *When waves enter shallow water, the water in them piles up until eventually they spill over at the top and break.*

- **If the fetch is short,** the waves may simply be a chaotic, choppy 'sea'. If the fetch is long, they may develop into a series of rolling waves called a swell.

- **One in 300,000 waves** is four times bigger than the rest.

- **The biggest waves** occur south of South Africa.

- **When waves** move into shallow water, the rolling of the water is impeded by the sea-bed. The water piles up, then spills over in a breaker.

Tsunamis

- **Tsunamis** are huge waves that begin when the sea floor is violently shaken by an earthquake, a landslide or a volcanic eruption.

- **In deep water** tsunamis travel almost unnoticeably below the surface. However, once they reach shallow coastal waters they rear up into waves 30 m high or higher.

- **Tsunamis** are often mistakenly called 'tidal waves', but they are nothing to do with tides. The word tsunami (soon-army) is Japanese for 'harbour wave'.

- **Tsunamis** usually come in a series of a dozen or more – anything from five minutes to one hour apart.

▼ *Tsunamis do little damage in open water but can cause huge amounts of damage in shallow waters and inland.*

A shift in the sea-bed sends out a pulse of water

As the pulse moves into shallow water it rears into a giant wave

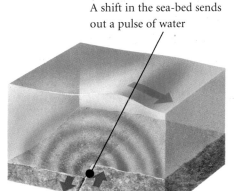 

▲ *Tsunamis may be generated underwater by an earthquake, then travel far along the sea-bed before emerging to swamp a coast.*

- **Before a tsunami arrives,** the sea may recede dramatically, like water draining from a bath.

- **Tsunamis can travel** along the sea-bed as fast as a jet plane, at 700 km/h or more.

- **Tsunamis** arrive within 15 minutes from a local quake.

- **A tsunami** generated by an earthquake in Japan might swamp San Francisco, USA, 10 hours later.

- **The biggest tsunami** ever recorded was an 85-m high wave which struck Japan on April 24, 1771.

- **Tsunami warnings** are issued by the Pacific Tsunami Warning Centre in Honolulu.

Tides

- **Tides are the way** the sea rises a little then falls back every 12 hours or so.

- **When the tide is flowing** it is rising. When the tide is ebbing it is falling.

- **Tides are caused** by the pull of gravity between the Earth, Moon and Sun.

- **The mutual pull** of the Moon's and the Earth's gravity stretches the Earth into an egg shape.

- **The solid Earth** is so rigid that it stretches only 20 cm.

- **Ocean waters** can flow freely over the Earth to create two tidal bulges (high tides) of water. One bulge is directly under the Moon, the other is on the far side of the Earth.

High tides happen at the same time each day on opposite sides of the Earth

▼ *At high tide, the sea rises up the shore and dumps seaweed, shells and drift wood. Most coasts have two high tides and two low tides every day.*

At high tide the water level rises

At low tide the water level goes down again

● **As the Earth rotates** every 24 hours the tidal bulges stay in the same place under the Moon. Each place on the ocean has high tide twice a day. The Moon is moving as well as the Earth, making high tides occur not once every 12 hours but once every 12 hours 25 minutes.

● **The continents** get in the way, making the tidal bulges slosh about in a complex way. As a result the timing and height of tides vary enormously. In the open ocean tides rise only 1 m or so, but in enclosed spaces such as the Bay of Fundy, in Nova Scotia, Canada they rise over 15 m.

● **The Sun is much farther away** than the Moon, but it is so big that its gravity has an effect on the tides.

● **The Moon and the Sun** line up at a Full and a New Moon, creating high spring tides twice a month. When the Moon and Sun pull at right angles at a Half Moon, they cause neap tides which are lower than normal tides.

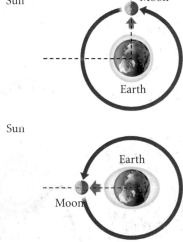

▶ *Neap tides occur when the Sun and Moon are at right angles to each other and pulling in different directions.*

▶ *Spring tides occur when the Sun and the Moon are lined up and pulling together.*

Ocean currents

▲ *Ocean currents start as wind blows across the water's surface.*

- **Ocean surface currents** are like giant rivers, often tens of kilometres wide, 100 m deep and flowing at 15 km/h.

- **The major currents** are split on either side of the Equator into giant rings called gyres.

- **In the Northern Hemisphere** the gyres flow round clockwise; in the south they flow anticlockwise.

- **Ocean currents** are driven by a combination of winds and the Earth's rotation.

● **Near the Equator** water is driven by easterly winds (see wind) to make westward-flowing equatorial currents.

● **When equatorial currents** reach continents, the Earth's rotation deflects them polewards as warm currents.

● **As warm currents flow** polewards, westerly winds drive them east back across the oceans. When the currents reach the far side, they begin to flow towards the Equator along the west coasts of continents as cool currents.

● **The North Atlantic Drift** brings so much warm water from the Caribbean to SW England that it is warm enough to grow palm trees, yet it is as far north as Newfoundland.

Wave movement

● **By drying out the air** cool currents can create deserts, such as California's Baja and Chile's Atacama deserts.

Surface currents

Underwater currents

▶ *The wind sets the surface waters in motion as currents. Waves create swirling circular currents, while deeper currents run beneath the surface.*

. . . .FASCINATING FACT. . . .
The West Wind Drift around Antarctica moves
2000 times as much water as the Amazon.

201

Deep ocean current

▲ *This satellite picture shows variations in ocean surface temperature.*

- **Ocean surface currents** (see ocean currents) affect only the top 100 m or so of the ocean. Deep currents involve the whole ocean.

- **Deep currents** are set in motion by differences in the density of sea water. They move only a few metres a day.

- **Most deep currents** are called thermohaline circulations because they depend on the water's temperature ('thermo') and salt content ('haline').

- **If seawater** is cold and salty, it is dense and sinks.

- **Typically, dense water** forms in the polar regions. Here the water is cold and weighed down by salt left behind when sea ice forms.

- **Dense polar water** sinks and spreads out towards the Equator deep below the surface.

- **Oceanographers** call dense water that sinks and starts deep ocean currents 'deep water'.

- **In the Northern Hemisphere** the main area for the formation of deep water is the North Atlantic.

- **Dense salty water** from the Mediterranean pours deep down very fast – 1 m per second – through the Straits of Gibraltar to add to the North Atlantic deep water.

- **There are three levels** in the ocean: the 'epilimnion' (the surface waters warmed by sunlight, up to 100–300 m down); the 'thermocline', where it becomes colder quickly with depth; and the 'hypolimnion', the bulk of deep, cold ocean water.

▲ *In the polar regions the waters become colder and saltier which makes them heavier. They sink and spread slowly toward the Equator.*

Ocean deeps

- **The oceans** are over 2000 m deep on average.

- **Along the edge** of the ocean is a ledge of land – the continental shelf. The average sea depth here is 130 m.

- **At the edge of the continental shelf** the sea-bed plunges thousands of metres steeply down the continental slope.

- **Underwater avalanches** roar down the continental slope at over 60 km/h. They carve out deep gashes called submarine canyons.

- **The gently** sloping foot of the continental slope is called the continental rise.

- **Beyond the continental rise** the ocean floor stretches out in a vast plain called the abyssal plain. It lies as deep as 5000 m below the water's surface.

▼ *Under the ocean there are mountains, plateau, plains and trenches similar to those found on land.*

Continental shelf

Continental slope

● **The abyssal plain** is covered in a thick slime called ooze. It is made partly from volcanic ash and meteor dust and partly from the remains of sea creatures.

● **The abyssal plain** is dotted with huge mountains, thousands of metres high, called seamounts.

● **Flat-topped seamounts** are called guyots. They may be volcanoes that once projected above the surface.

● **The deepest places** in the ocean floor are ocean trenches – made when tectonic plates are driven down into the mantle. The Mariana Trench is 10,863 m deep.

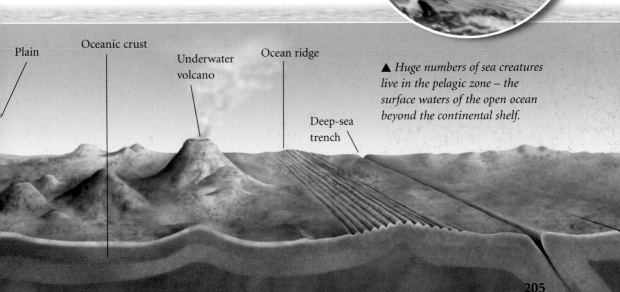

Plain

Oceanic crust

Underwater volcano

Ocean ridge

Deep-sea trench

▲ *Huge numbers of sea creatures live in the pelagic zone – the surface waters of the open ocean beyond the continental shelf.*

205

Black smokers

▲ *Black smokers were first discovered less than 30 years ago.*

- **Black smokers** are natural chimneys on the sea-bed. They billow black fumes of hot gases and water.

- **Black smokers** are technically known as hydrothermal vents. They are volcanic features.

- **Black smokers** form along mid-ocean ridges where the tectonic plates are moving apart.

- **Black smokers** begin when seawater seeps through cracks in the sea floor. The water is heated by volcanic magma, and it dissolves minerals from the rock.

206

- **Once the water is superheated,** it spews from the vents in scalding, mineral-rich black plumes.

- **The plume cools** rapidly in the cold sea, leaving behind thick deposits of sulphur, iron, zinc and copper in tall, chimney-like vents.

- **The tallest vents** are 50 m high.

- **Water jetting** from black smokers can reach 662°C.

- **Smokers** are home to a community of organisms that thrive in the scalding waters and toxic chemicals. The organisms include giant clams and tube worms.

▶ *Over 2500 m below the surface black smokers spew out hot water, black with mineral-rich mud. Around them grow tubeworms, some as long as cars.*

. . . FASCINATING FACT . . .
Each drop of sea water in the world circulates through a smoker every ten million years.

207

Index

Index

Index

Index

Index

Index

Index

Acknowledgements

The publishers would like to thank the following
artists who have contributed to this book:

Gary Hincks, Janos Marffy, Guy Smith

The publishers would like to thank the following
sources for the use of their photographs:

Page 30 Lloyd Cluff/CORBIS; Page 39 Jeremy Horner/CORBIS;
Page 66 Morton Beebe S.F./CORBIS; Page 68 Michael S Yamashita/CORBIS;
Page 206 Ralph White/CORBIS

All other pictures from the Miles Kelly Archives.